Unsung Heroes of Texas

Ann Ruff

Enjoy the best of Texas with these Lone Star Books:

Unsung Heroes of Texas

Ann Ruff

*Stories of courage and honor
from
Texas history and legend*

Lone Star Books
A Division of Gulf Publishing Company
Houston, Texas

Dedication

For William J. Lowe, another of my heroes.

Library of Congress Cataloging-in-Publication Data

Ruff, Ann, 1930–
  Unsung heroes of Texas.

  Includes index.
  1. Texas—Biography. 2. Texas—History, Local.
I. Title.
CT262.R83   1985   976.4   85-17606

ISBN 0-88415-864-0

Illustrations by Roxann L. Combs

Photo Credits

Abbott, Pat, p. 123
Barker Texas History Center, The University of Texas at
    Austin
  Etta-Adele Martin Collection, p. 5
  Louis W. Kemp Papers, p. 36
  Oral History of the Texas Oil Industry, p. 97
  Texas Collection Photograph Files, pp. 29, 32, 71, 118
Clark, James A., and Halbouty, Michel T., *Spindletop*, Gulf
    Publishing Co., Houston, 1980, p. 91
Cravens, Logan, Austin, pp. 99, 111
East Texas Oil and Gas Museum, Kilgore, p. 95
Fuller, B. F., *History of Texas Baptists*, Baptist Book Concern,
    Louisville, Kentucky, 1900 (in Texas State Archives,
    Austin), p. 43
Kelly, Dayton, Salado (copy courtesy of the Institute of
    Texan Cultures, San Antonio), p. 104
Montana Historical Society, p. 51

Patterson, Mildred, Bend, p. 89
Ruff, Ann, Llano, pp. 50, 80
Ruff, Ann, *The Alamo and Other Texas Missions to Remember*,
    Gulf Publishing Co., Houston, 1984, p. 1
Seeliger, Weldon, Llano, p. 112
Smith, A. Morton, *The First 100 Years in Cooke County*, The
    Naylor Company, San Antonio, 1955 (in the Texas State
    Archives, Austin), 48
Smithsonian Institution Photo No. 1746-A-2, p.65
Sowell, A. J., *Early Settlers and Indian Fighters of Southwest
    Texas*, Argosy-Antiquarian, Ltd., New York (in the
    Barker Texas History Center, The University of Texas
    at Austin), p. 68
Texas Highways, Austin, p. 19
Western History Collections Library of The University of
    Oklahoma, Norman, Noah H. Rose Collection, p. 108

Contents

VI. Frontier Justice and Mercy

VII. Heroes of the Oil Patch

VIII. Visionaries, Missionaries, and Entrepreneurs

Acknowledgments

This was a difficult book to research, and I am deeply indebted to the very kind and helpful ladies at the Llano County Public Library. For a small library, they had a very good Texana section.

I also wish to thank the wonderful people at the State Archives in Austin and the Barker Library at the University of Texas in Austin. The Texas Room of the Houston Public Library was a treasure of information, as was the Panhandle Plains Museum in Canyon. And I could not have done without Sue and Weldon Seeliger of Llano; Pat Abbott of Kerrville; Mildred Patterson of Bend; Mrs. Walter Lang of Castell; the Timmerman sisters of Geronimo; Joe White, director of Kilgore's East Texas Oil Museum; Logan Cravens of Austin; the Comanche Chamber of Commerce; the *Amarillo Daily Tribune*; the Pioneer Memorial Library in Fredericksburg; Brazoria County's Historical Society; Dr. Stanley Siegel, University of Houston; and the Fort Worth Public Library. These too, are the unsung heroes that made this book possible.

Introduction

The true heroes of Texas are not just those men and women whose names are found emblazoned on monuments and recorded in history books. Thousands of Texans labored, fought, and died for their state and its people in obscurity and without recognition. I learned of some of these unknown heroes when a motorcycle buddy and I covered a lot of Texas miles on our bikes and spent a considerable amount of time reading historical markers along the way. The markers would often describe some momentous event and briefly refer to a character no one had ever heard of before. One such marker recounted the Goliad Massacre and mentioned The Angel of Goliad. She was a brave woman who had saved the lives of many Texans on that black day, but she never made the history books. She was only a line on a historical marker already crowded with names, and one of many Texans mentioned on such markers, whose heroic deeds are relatively unknown. Being the avid history buff that I am, I convinced Bill Lowe of Gulf Publishing Company that these unsung heroes deserved some lyrics of their own.

Finding unknown heroes was no problem. I first picked up Claude Dooley's book *Why Stop? A Guide to Texas Historical Roadside Markers* (also published by Gulf Publishing) and read every single entry, and that is a lot of historical markers. Although historical markers can be incredibly dry and lacking in colorful detail, I tried to pick out events and characters that I thought would make a great story. Next I spent a lot of time digging in the Texas collections of libraries around the state. Other history buffs who learned about my project would ask if I was including their favorite unsung hero and send me what information they had. A bit of serendipity was also involved. As I was researching one hero, another, more heroic person whose life was intertwined with the first would sometimes appear. For example, I had planned to include Sion T. Bostick as the captor of

Santa Anna, but found out the real hero was James A. Sylvester. (Those readers who wonder why Emily Morgan, the slave girl who entertained Santa Anna before the Battle of San Jacinto, is not included should remember that the Yellow Rose of Texas is a very sung-about heroine.)

Finally, this book began to take shape as a way to help readers appreciate Texas history from a different slant. Major events such as the battles of the Alamo, Goliad, and San Jacinto provided a framework from which to tell the Texas story from the viewpoint of little-known men and women who acted with courage, never dreaming they would contribute to the destiny of a great state. These people were not seeking glory or immortality—they were merely acting in accordance with their beliefs. No eternal flames burn in their memory, few monuments rise in their honor, and most died forgotten.

In some ways this is a sad book, and your heart will break when you read the tragic ends of some heroes such as Robert Neighbors, Chief Bowles, and Alfred Hayne. Yet, in another way these stories of Texans dedicated to a cause or a deed they sincerely believed in make this an inspiring book. It did not matter to them that they received little or no recognition, and most would probably be astounded to find themselves described as heroes today. That attitude and their actions are what make these men and women the truly unsung heroes of Texas.

I
Before the Storm

The First Republic

Bernardo Gutierrez
de Lara
San Antonio, 1812

F OR THREE CENTURIES SPAIN had slumbered and a conquered Mexico seethed with revolution. The vast territory of northern Mexico was ignored and considered fit only for wild savages, for Coronado had proved there was no gold. Yet, some empire builders did yearn to control this unknown wilderness. These *filibusters* (or *freebooters*) were the precursors of the revolutionaries who formed the Republic of Texas. Although doomed to failure, these men with dreams of glory served to set the stage for the final act of independence on the battlefield of San Jacinto.

Webster defines a filibuster as an adventurer who engages in a private military action in a foreign country. From the Spanish *filibustero* and the French *filibustier,* or pirate, the label is aptly applied to the colorful, ambitious men who envisioned Texas as their own domain. But endless horizons and undisciplined armies defeated the best laid plans of these dreamers of wealth and power. Philip Nolan, Dr. James Long, and even Aaron Burr had designs for an empire west of the Sabine. These visionaries were far ahead of their time, but the only filibuster who had any degree of success was Bernardo Gutierrez de Lara.

In 1810 when Father Hidalgo challenged Mexico to assert her independence with his famous *Grito de Dolores,* the revolutionists sent one of their staunchest members, Gutierrez de Lara, to Philadelphia to plead their cause and enlist the aid of the United States. Here Gutierrez met Jose Alvarez de Toledo, a Spanish refugee also plotting to overthrow the Royalist government of Mexico. The two became involved, sharing a common cause, but Gutierrez pursued the goal with more zeal.

By 1812 de Lara was in Natchitoches, Louisiana, recruiting an army for the invasion of Texas. A brilliant West Point graduate, Augustus Magee, had been extremely successful in keeping down the robberies and murders in this wild and lawless Neutral Zone, but he had been passed over for promotion. The disgruntled Magee was an eager and ideal leader for a sortie into Texas.

On August 8, 1812, the Gutierrez-Magee Expedition crossed the Sabine, and this Republican Army of the North was welcomed with open arms at Nacogdoches, always a hotbed of anti-Spanish and later anti-Mexican sentiment. Men from good families, idealists, more than a few drifters, and even some Indians joined the motley army—for $40 a month and a league of land.

With Magee in command the rebels surprised the Spanish troops at La Bahia and captured the presidio. Then Magee died in January of 1813 under circumstances shrouded in mystery. An ex-tavern owner, Samuel Kemper, took over and marched the army to San Antonio de Bexar, where he defeated the Spanish troops. Kemper demanded and received an unconditional surrender, and the green flag of the Republic flew over Bexar.

Gutierrez now began to assume control. His field was politics rather than warfare. On April 6, 1813, years of work, scheming, and plotting had come to fruition, and Texas was declared an independent nation. What a glorious triumph it was!

Victory, however, was fleeting. Gutierrez made a tragic error. He allowed his Captain Delgado to cut the throats of the captured Royalist generals Herra and Salcedo. Once again the Spanish and Anglo cultures clashed, with Kemper infuriated by the senseless murders. Taking with him 100 Americans, Kemper left "on furlough." With a good portion of the Americans gone, the new Republic was doomed.

Toledo had not been idle those years that Gutierrez had been working for Mexican liberation from Spain. He, too, had his own plans for glory and they did not include de Lara. Toledo arrived at Bexar just as two forces of Spanish Royalists under Generals Elizondo and Arredondo were marching to recapture San Antonio. The clever Toledo convinced Gutierrez's Mexican junta, the government of the Texas Republic, that unless he replaced Gutierrez as their leader the remaining Americans would leave.

Gutierrez was cast out in spite of his impassioned pleas to be allowed to remain until after the forthcoming battle with Arredondo. The leader of the first successful defeat of Spanish forces in their New World territories saw his dreams destroyed. There was nothing left for the downhearted man to do but return to Nacogdoches. The hero was gone, and in his place was the pompous Toledo. The achievements of de Lara's years of effort were annihilated in a brief fourteen days.

Yet, those years 1811–1813 were a proud chapter in the history of Texas. Not only had Texas been the first colony to achieve independence from Spain, but it was also the first to establish an opposing force within its environs. The Texans themselves had suffered and fought bravely for an ideal that Texans have held dearly since then—the ideal of freedom and self rule.

As for the cast of characters in this tragic play of independence: Kemper returned to his tavern and steadfastly refused to take part in the other filibustering attempts. Gutierrez tried again to revive his lost cause with James Long's expedition into Texas, which also failed. Ironically, the rebel ended his career as governor of the state of Tamaulipaz after Emperor Iturbide of Mexico recognized the efforts Gutierrez had made on behalf of independence.

In the Battle of Medina against Elizondo and Arredondo, Toledo made the tactical error of putting Indians and Mexicans in one division and Americans in the other. His army lacked unity, and he was soundly defeated. His troops were slaughtered, many shot in retribution for the murders of Herra and Salcedo. Toledo was spared, and by a curious twist of fate he made his own peace with Spain. In the years before his death Toledo advised Spanish ministers on how to suppress revolution in the colonies.

There was one other character in this sad drama that should be mentioned. As a result of the Royalist victory at Medina, one of Arredondo's officers always considered San Antonio lucky for him. His name was Antonio Lopez de Santa Anna.

As for Texas, from 1814–1821 it became a veritable asylum for adventurers, pirates, and filibusters. No wonder Stephen F. Austin described his future home as "a howling wilderness."

Friend of the Empresarios

Baron Felipe Enrique Neri de Bastrop San Antonio de Bexar, 1823

HISTORY IS FILLED WITH fortuitous accidents that have changed the course of events, and the destiny of Texas was shaped by just such an accidental meeting.

It was a discouraged and downhearted Moses Austin that left Governor Antonio Maria Martinez's office that bitter December day in 1820. Not only had the governor refused to hear his petition to bring colonists to Texas, but Martinez had ordered him to leave Spanish territory. All Austin's hard and tedious efforts had been in vain. There was no hope of ever bringing his grand scheme of settling Texas to fruition.

As the frustrated empresario plodded the streets of Bexar, he happened to run into an old acquaintance he had known some years before in Louisiana, Baron Felipe Enrique Neri de Bastrop. The pleasure of seeing a

Stephen F. Austin's colonization of Texas hinged on his fateful meeting with the Baron de Bastrop (seated at table).

familiar face quickly left Austin's heart as his bitter disappointment returned. As the two friends shared a refreshment, Austin told Bastrop about the governor's unconditional refusal to listen to his plea and the order to leave Spanish land forever. Then, to Austin's extreme good fortune, Bastrop offered to be of service to him. The baron was personally acquainted with Martinez and would secure an audience for the Missourian.

The two entrepreneurs prepared a scheme for the introduction of 300 families of good character into Texas, describing them to Martinez as being faithful Spanish subjects who had remained in Louisiana after Spain had relinquished control of the land east of the Sabine. Now that Louisiana was no longer part of Spain, they wished to move west to Spanish territory. This was not true, but it sounded good and was perhaps just what Martinez might accept.

The ploy worked. With the Baron's intervention, Moses Austin was not only granted an interview, but the governor forwarded his petition to General Joaquin de Arredondo, chief civil and military commandant of Texas, at Monterrey. On Jan. 17, 1821, Arredondo approved a grant permitting Austin to settle his 300 families within an area of 200,000 acres. Terms of Austin's grant were very vague, even its location was unspecified. No provision was made for administration, nor was Austin's title defined. All Moses Austin knew was he had 200,000 acres in Texas, thanks to his friend, Baron de Bastrop.

You can't help but wonder what would have happened if Moses Austin had not met de Bastrop. Would another *empresario* have accomplished Austin's scheme for Texas, or would colonization have been delayed for so long that Mexico would have established a firm foothold in her vast territory?

With his dreams of an empire in Texas almost within his reach, however, the great empresario died. It would be his son, Stephen Fuller Austin, who would become "The Father of Texas."

Stephen learned of his father's death as he waited for him in Natchitoches, Louisiana. There was nothing left for the young man to do but carry out his father's plan. So in August of 1821 Stephen F. Austin presented himself to Governor Martinez. The governor was very impressed with young Austin's poise and obvious ambition, but there was one problem. At this time Austin did not speak Spanish. Once again Baron de Bastrop came to the rescue of the Texas cause and became the translator for the serious business of colonizing Texas.

The terms were for Austin to explore the coastal plain between the San Antonio and Brazos Rivers and select a site. There would be 640 acres for each man, 320 for his wife, 160 acres per child, and 80 acres per slave. Austin could also collect twelve and one-half cents per acre to compensate for the survey and title. The colonists had a year to make improvements to the land, and they had to take the oath of allegiance. Austin was responsible for their good conduct.

At last! Every detail seemed set for the first 300 families to enter Texas. Then the Mexican Revolution occurred. Austin was forced to go to Mexico City and present his cause once again to the Mexican government. As always, the turbulence in Mexican politics caused delay after delay. Finally, on April 14, 1823, Mexico made the most fateful single act in its history with the approval of legal colonization in Texas under Stephen F. Austin. For by 1836 it was plain which of the two nations had become the stronger. Texas, with her 20,000 Anglos, had held against 9 million Mexicans, and the Mexican point of view ceased to be of great significance in Texas.

Austin's colonists had already entered Texas in 1821 sub rosa, but not until 1823 were they there legally. By the time other *empresarios* were ready for their share of Texas, Austin had had a four-year headstart.

With colonization legal, the Mexican government needed to send in a land commissioner to collect fees, particularly from the squatters who had moved in during the turmoil of Mexico's revolution. Who should be the land commissioner but none other than the Baron de Bastrop, just as Moses and the Baron had planned. Now, in agreement with Stephen F. Austin, the land commissioner charged $127 a league for signing the titles, and he shared his fees with Austin.

The Baron arrived to find a disheartened group of new Texans. They were victims of sickness, Indians, thieves, and every pioneer hardship that existed. They were truly a sullen lot, who felt Mexico had deserted them. Most of the miserable pioneers were on the verge of returning to the United States. After the Baron listened to their woes, he used his gift of eloquence to convince the colonists of the constancy of the Mexican government and its interest in protecting them. So convincing was his presentation, the settlers resolved to stay. The Baron had helped Austin save his colony again.

The settlers were so impressed with Bastrop they elected him to the provincial deputation at Bexar which was to choose a representative to the legislature of the newly created state of Coahuila. The Baron was selected and moved to the capital of Coahuila (of which Texas was a part), the bustling and ancient town of Saltillo. Here he worked tirelessly for the Texas colonists.

Until his death in 1827, the Baron sought legislation favorable to the cause of immigration and in the interest of the settlers. He secured passage of the Colonization Act of 1827; and he was instrumental in the passage of an act establishing a port at Galveston.

Clearly Bastrop was a true champion of the Texas cause, but little is known about him. His background was suspect and his past shrouded in mystery. One source states that he had been a Prussian soldier of fortune under Frederick the Great and later a soldier in the service of the King of Spain who sent him to Mexico. Another historian believed Bastrop was a French nobleman, yet officials of the Spanish Foreign Office were convinced he was an adventurer from the United States. According to Bastrop's own story, in his last will and testament, dated January 16, 1827, he was born of nobility in Holland about 1766. Who he really was hardly matters. The fact is that he did Texas invaluable service from that fateful meeting in 1820 until he died.

As so often is the case, Texas did not repay Bastrop for his services. According to the Mexican system, he was to be paid by contributions from his constituents. The contributions were far from generous. Bastrop did not even leave enough money to pay his burial expenses, and his fellow legislators donated the funds for his funeral. Nor is he even buried in the state he served so unfailingly, but rather in a forgotten grave in Saltillo. Only a small Texas town bears his name. Stephen F. Austin may be called the Father of Texas, but it was this little-remembered friend of Texas that made that honor possible.

Padre of Texas

ON A BACKROAD TO nowhere lies a tiny hamlet called Muldoon. A country store, a dinky post office, and the remnants of a strange stone structure of uncertain origin are the only remains of the town named for "The Forgotten Man of Texas History," Father Miguel Muldoon. Even the small monument erected to his memory by private citizens is no longer here. It was moved to the side of Highway 77, a few miles south of LaGrange.

Why was the good padre forgotten? Possibly the Texas colonists associated him with a religion distasteful to them because of its direct connection to Mexican authority. When Mexico made its fateful decision to allow the Anglos into Texas, it erroneously believed that converting the new

Father Miguel Muldoon Muldoon, 1831

settlers to Catholicism would ensure their loyalty to Mexico. Therefore, one of the provisions of colonization was that all Anglos must accept the Catholic faith. To minister to their spiritual needs, at the request of Stephen F. Austin, Mexico sent the new Texans Padre Miguel Muldoon. The colonists may not have wished to embrace Catholicism, but Texas was indeed fortunate in Austin's choice, for Muldoon would prove one of Texas' strongest friends.

Muldoon's background is somewhat vague and cloudy. His father was a native of Ireland, but after a fight with a British soldier, the Irishman fled to Spain and married a Spanish girl. Their son, Miguel, was given an excellent education and trained for the priesthood. The young man's love of adventure caused him to go to Mexico in 1821 as chaplain to Don Juan D'Donojo, the last viceroy of Spain. Somehow he managed to remain in Mexico even after the Spanish were overthrown.

While Stephen F. Austin was in Mexico working for his grant in Texas, he had the good luck to meet Muldoon. The two became fast friends. Not only did the good padre teach Austin Spanish, he loaned the empresario money. The two struck a bargain. In return for ministry to his flock, Austin would pay the curate 11 leagues of land (48,610 acres).

Muldoon arrived in San Felipe in April of 1831. This big, red-faced man, although often pugnacious and drunken, was also golden hearted. He made the colonists Catholics on an assembly-line basis and never insisted that his "Muldoon Catholics" take their new religion seriously. (Stephen F. Austin never became a Catholic at all.) The jovial priest staged the wedding of all weddings when he married thirty people at one time. The feast lasted two days and nights, and the one who celebrated the most was Father Muldoon. Muldoon tended his duties with laughter on his lips and often requested only a jug of spirits for his services. On his rangy mule, Muldoon rode through his huge parish as sort of a Texas version of Friar Tuck.

Muldoon also had a deep concern for his Texas friends. When Indians kidnapped a woman and her two children, Muldoon made a solitary trip into the hostile Comanche territory and succeeded in rescuing the mother, although the children were lost. Only a priest who loved his fellow man more than his life would have undertaken such a dangerous task.

During those years of prelude to the Revolution, Muldoon offered his aid many times to Texas. In 1832 when Juan David Bradburn, the hated Mexican commander of Anahuac, imprisoned Patrick Jack and William B. Travis, Muldoon went with John Austin and the angry colonists to liberate their fellow Texans. Two years later Muldoon was in Mexico when Stephen F. Austin was thrown in jail for telling the Mexican government that Texas should be a separate state and not a part of Coahuila. It was Miguel Muldoon who helped secure Austin's release.

Muldoon's two best friends were John and William Wharton. After the Battle of San Jacinto it was imperative that the United States recognize the Republic of Texas. William Wharton was Texas' first minister to the United States to secure that recognition. In 1837, on Wharton's return, he was captured at sea by two Mexican gunboats and imprisoned in Matamoros.

Muldoon went immediately to the aid of his friend and to the aid of Texas. The clever padre bribed the guards and smuggled Wharton out of prison in a priest's robe. Muldoon told his friend, "If you are accosted, simply extend your right hand with the first two fingers elevated and say, 'Pax Vobiscum.' Remember, you are a Catholic priest until you reach Texas." Wharton escaped in time to be elected to the Texas Senate, thanks to Miguel Muldoon.

In many ways Muldoon was a man of mystery. He swept into the affairs of Texas and then suddenly dropped out of sight. No one knows if a vengeful Santa Anna sought retribution or if Muldoon was allowed to return to Spain. It is hoped the good father spent the rest of his life with his favorite jug in the Spanish sun remembering his exciting days in that wild new land of Texas.

A Lifetime of Loyalty

ON APRIL 14, 1823, Mexico made the most fateful single act in its history with the approval of legal colonization in Texas under Stephen F. Austin. About the only thing the Anglos and the Mexicans had in common was that they both wanted Texas. By the early 1830s the differences of opinions between the two cultures were manifested in outbreaks of violence.

Colonel David Kokernot Anahuac, 1832

At the tiny customs port of Anahuac the Mexican garrison was commanded by an American, Colonel John David Bradburn, who had joined the Mexican Army. He was totally despised by the colonists because he had purchased supplies locally and refused to pay for them.

A young attorney named William B. Travis was aiding a Louisiana planter in getting back two runaway slaves now employed by Bradburn. Without apparent reason, Travis and his friend Patrick Jack were thrown in prison. (According to some accounts it was because Jack and Travis gave Bradburn a hot foot during a parade.) William Jack, Patrick's brother, called for help, and 150 men rallied to demand release of the prisoners. While part of the volunteers marched to Anahuac, the rest went to Brazoria to get a cannon to free "the gallant young men from the calaboose."

The cannon was acquired, and then the group formulated plans to blockade the port. It could hardly be called a fleet, but in 1832 the first Texas Navy was organized. Its three ships were the *Water Witch, Red Rover,* and *Stephen F. Austin.* The *Stephen F. Austin* was five tons with five guns and five men commanded by David Kokernot. Kokernot and his "fleet" successfully blockaded the port and even captured three boats loaded with all sorts of food.

Mexican troops arrived at Anahuac, and Travis and Jack were released. However, the "navy" sailed on to Galveston and captured the customs house, loaded their vessels, and returned home. None were punished. This was the year all Mexican troops in Texas were going back to Mexico to declare themselves for Santa Anna in his takeover of the current Mexican government. Only one small garrison was left in San Antonio. At this time even the Texans sided with Santa Anna.

The "battle" at Anahuac had been exciting, and the colonists had won the first round, but David Kokernot continued to serve the rebel cause with all of his heart. His was not a single act of heroism, but a lifetime of continued unswerving duty. A few years after Anahuac Kokernot made a trip to Nacogdoches, and his encounter with Sam Houston would shape his destiny. Kokernot wrote:

> As I walked up the street I noticed the finest looking man I ever saw seated on the steps of Col. Thorn's store. He was dressed in a complete Indian costume made of buckskin and ornamented with a profuse variety of beads, and his massive head was covered with a fine broad beaver hat.

After exchanging pleasantries the two men settled down to a glass of wine to discuss the seriousness of those days in 1834. Kokernot recalled the conversation.

> "Now, my friend," said the General, "tell me the news."
> I replied, "The news is war. It is rumored that Santa Anna is gathering troops to send into Texas to disarm the inhabitants, but we are determined not to surrender our arms."
> "Well, my friend," said the General, "how will you act in that case?"
> I again replied with seriousness, "We will fight them to the last, or die in the attempt."
> "Who will command the army?" he asked.
> My answer was, "My dear sir, if I had the authority to make the appointment, you are the man, for you are the finest looking man I ever laid eyes on."

He immediately replied, "Well, my dear sir, if I get the appointment of commander I will give you a commission."

Then he pulled out a small pocketbook and wrote my name. Then we shook hands and bade each other farewell. From that day I loved Sam Houston. He proved a friend indeed.

Finally, in the fall of 1835 the call came that Texas had been waiting for. They would march against the invading army of General Cos, brother-in-law to Santa Anna. Kokernot mustered ten men and set off for Gonzales. Here by acclamation Stephen F. Austin was elected Commander-in-Chief of the little band of 100 patriots. On their march to San Antonio, Kokernot served his Republic once more. The famous scout Deaf Smith had been sent to San Antonio to spy out the city, and but for the intervention of Kokernot a picket might have shot him. As Kokernot told the story:

One of our pickets hailed him three times to no purpose. But, seeing Smith's movements I surmised that it might be our faithful spy and stopped the picket just as he put his hand on the trigger to fire at the deaf man who had not heard him.

A day later at the Battle of Conception, 1,000 Mexicans attacked the 82 Texans. Bowie and Travis exhibited the utmost coolness and bravery and at three o'clock that afternoon the enemy retreated leaving 120 dead. The Texans lost but one man.

On the fifth of December Colonel Milam called for volunteers to take San Antonio. David Kokernot was among the first willing to fight. There were 1,500 Mexicans against 400 Texans, and the battle raged for 4 days. It was with great sadness that Kokernot saw the death of Ben Milam. Finally Cos surrendered to Burleson, and the campaign of 1835 was over. The tired and weary Texans went home—leaving Travis and Bowie at the Alamo.

David Kokernot was to offer his life again for the Texas cause. On March 5, 1836, he received a letter saying "Independence is declared! It must be maintained! Immediate action united with valor, that alone can achieve the great work. The services of all are forthwith required in the field." It was signed "Sam Houston, Commander-in-Chief of the Army." On March 6, Kokernot mounted his mustang pony and once again rode to Gonzales. Houston had not forgotten his young admirer that day in Nacogdoches. It was now *Captain* David Kokernot that hurried to his general's aid.

The new captain arrived in Gonzales to be greeted with the tale of terror carried by Mrs. Dickenson to Sam Houston about the fall of the Alamo. The Texas Army's retreat and final victory is history, but Captain David Kokernot never faltered in his trust of Houston's decisions.

Even after San Jacinto, there was one last duty for Captain Kokernot. In Santa Anna's captured papers Houston found the names of prominent Texas Tories. Many of these collaborators had relatives who had fought bravely for the rebels, so out of wisdom and kindness Houston sent Captain Kokernot to inform the known Tories along and beyond the Trinity River they were now working for a lost cause. Kokernot never revealed any of the names and his discretion helped unify a struggling Republic.

His Heart Was True Blue

**William Goyens
Nacogdoches, 1835**

IT IS BEAUTIFUL IN the spring on Goyens Hill. Dogwood and wild azaleas add their special touch of loveliness to the dark pines of East Texas. The magnificent mansion that once stood here is gone now, but many years ago in another time stood the home of one of the wealthiest men in Texas—a man who was also a mulatto.

Goyens came to Texas in 1821 from North Carolina. His father was a free mulatto and his mother was white. Little is known of his early years, but when Bill arrived in Nacogdoches, he was seventeen and could only write his name. It was only a few years before this highly intelligent young man could write English and Spanish and speak a number of Indian dialects including Cherokee and Comanche.

One of Texas' first industries was begun in Nacogdoches when Bill Goyens established a blacksmith shop and became a wagon manufacturer. Ironically, Goyens himself owned slaves that worked in his wagon shop. In addition to this lucrative business, Goyens operated a freight line into Louisiana and built a sawmill and gristmill on his hundreds of acres of land. For sport and pleasure this rich businessman had a string of race-horses.

Life was not easy for a man of Goyens' background in a predominately white land. Once, a few years after his arrival in Texas on a freighting trip to Natchitoches, Louisiana, the youth was seized by a William English who sought to sell him into slavery. For his freedom Goyens had to deliver to English his Negro slave woman and sign himself into peonage (although Goyens did receive the right to trade in his own behalf). After his return to Nacogdoches, the canny Goyens filed suit for annulment of this obligation and won.

In a court of law, this successful mulatto had no equal. For his own survival in a society where such a role was usually reserved for whites, Goyens became an expert in Mexican law, then the law of the Republic of Texas, and finally the State of Texas legal codes. His great friends Sam Houston and Thomas J. Rusk, both lawyers, were a source of strength to Goyens, for there were many litigations in which white men tried to take his land. "Mr. Goyens," as Houston always addressed his friend, was well respected.

Goyens' greatest service to the Republic was his role as Indian agent for the Cherokees. (Some sources say he acted as Houston's interpreter when the treaty with Chief Bowles was negotiated, but Houston had lived many years with the Cherokees and certainly did not need an interpreter with his old friends.) During the Revolution, it was Goyens who worked with the Cherokees to keep the tribe on the side of Texas. How it must have pained Goyens when the Cherokees were forced from their lands after the revolution. The treaty he had worked so hard with Houston to negotiate ended up absolutely worthless for the dispossesed Indians.

Bill Goyens married a white woman, Mary Pate Sibley, which in those years must have taken a great deal of courage. He built her a beautiful mansion on a hill overlooking Moral Creek, and when Bill Goyens died in 1856 he was buried beside his wife not far from Goyens Hill. For the Centennial the State of Texas erected a marker over his grave. There are a few errors in the facts of Bill's life, but the sentiment is there with the epitaph:

> His skin was black,
> His heart true blue.

As an added postscript to Goyen's list of achievements, the solid opposition to black ownership of land in post-revolutionary Texas broke down with the passage of a bill in the Senate authorizing Goyens to apply for the post of land commissioner and secure a certificate for a league and a labor of land (more than 4,000 acres) to which he was entitled.

The First Whose Blood Was Shed

THE BATTLE OF GOLIAD wasn't much of a battle. The big excitement had been a controversy over a cannon at nearby Gonzales where defiant Texans had challenged the Mexican Army to "come and take it." Captain George M. Collingsworth in his report on the battle at Goliad the morning of October 10, 1835 wrote "I arrived

**Samuel McCulloch
Goliad, 1835**

here last night at 11 o'clock and marched into the fort by forcing the church doors; and after a small fight they surrendered with three officers and twenty-one soldiers, together with three wounded and one killed. I had one of my men wounded in the shoulder."

Wounded in the Battle of Goliad was Samuel McCulloch, a free Negro, who described himself as "the first whose blood was shed in the war for independence." McCulloch paid dearly for this unique distinction, as his shattered shoulder left him a helpless invalid for nearly a year and a cripple for life.

The Battle of Goliad did give the Texans control over supplies from Copano Bay to San Antonio. The original plan had been to attack General Cos before he could reach Bexar, but most of the Texas men heeded the call from Gonzales. Cos embarked at Copano Bay, marched to Goliad, left thirty men and supplies and went on to Bexar. Collingsworth's company of Texans refused to be diverted from their primary aim, and forty-nine "good and effective" men signed a pledge to "take up the line of march for Goliad." Goliad remained in Texas hands until the Fannin Massacre the next year.

In 1837 the House of Representatives of the Republic received a petition begging special privileges from Samuel McCulloch. McCulloch outlined his services in the army, and stated that under the laws of Mexico he had been a citizen but that he had never made application for any land. Since the war he had "by marriage become the head of a family." He continued that he was "desirous of settling in life and performing the duties of a citizen, but he unhappily finds that by the Laws of the Country, for the Independence of which he has fought and bled, and still suffers, he is deprived of citizenship by reason of an unfortunate admixture of African blood, which he is said, without any fault of his, to inherit from a remote maternal ancestor. Since he could not receive the land to which he believed himself entitled without the beneficent action of Congress, he prayed for that action and for the privilege of remaining in Texas with his children." The committee on claims and accounts to whom McCulloch's petition was referred rejected his plea for land and citizenship, but not for residence rights.

The next year the freedman did receive one league of land (4,428 acres) because he was a permanently disabled veteran, but citizenship and his headright were still denied. McCulloch and his family were also exempted from the act of February 1840 which required all free blacks to leave the Republic. When Texas went to war for independence and freedom, it did not include freedom for blacks, nor did it include recognition of free Negroes as citizens.

In the summer of 1840 the Comanches swept down the Guadalupe killing settlers and stealing horses. It was a massive raid, one of the largest depredations in Texas. The Texans, organized under General Felix Huston, Colonel Edward Burleson, and Captain Mathew Caldwell, won a decisive victory over the Comanches at Plum Creek. The dreaded Comanche would never raid that far into Texas again. There, fighting valiantly against the Indians was Samuel McCulloch.

In 1842 Mexico made an abortive attempt to regain Texas, or at least a part of it. Santa Anna's friend, General Adrian Woll, marched on San Antonio with a thousand men. His attack was successful and San Antonio once again capitulated to the Mexican army. Woll's victory was short-lived, however, and within a few weeks the general had retreated back to Mexico. A spy was sent to San Antonio to ascertain Woll's strength. That spy had been Samuel McCulloch.

In spite of McCulloch's willingness to fight and die for Texas, it took the Negro until 1858 to recieve his headright. It was not until Texas was a state that Samuel McCulloch became a full-fledged citizen. The historian, William Physick Zuber, described McCulloch as "generally recognized as an honorable white man and treated as such." But it was not until twenty-three years had passed.

Father of the Texas Declaration of Independence

I N SO MANY INCIDENTS, the Texas Revolution seems a replay of the American Revolution. In the American unheaval the "shot heard round the world" was fired at Lexington in April of 1775, but it was July of 1776 before the colonies made their Declaration of Independence. After the "shot heard round the bayou" at Gonzales, there was

George Campbell
Childress
Washington-
on-the-Brazos, 1836

Like many of Texas' heroes, the Father of the Texas Declaration of Independence, George Campbell Childress, ended his life by suicide.

continual fighting, but for some reason the Texans seemed reluctant to proclaim their independence. From the time the men of Gonzales defied General Urgartechea to "come and take it" in October of 1835 until the actual Declaration of Independence, six months elapsed.

During those indecisive days there was a provisional government and a general legislative council called the Consultation. If one word is used to describe the provisional government, it would be "fractious." Governor Henry Smith and Lieutenant Governor James Robinson were extremely difficult to get along with, and there was constant uproar and turmoil. Texans were showing they could not govern themselves and were merely typical frontiersmen.

Finally, a call for a convention to meet March 1, 1836, was issued. All logic dictated that they *must* declare independence. The United States would not send aid unless Texas made its intentions clear. No one in the States wanted to finance a civil war, but if Texas declared independence, then the big financiers might be willing to gamble in return for large grants of Texas soil. This was similar to France telling Benjamin Franklin during the American Revolution there would be no alliance unless the colonies declared themselves free.

Probably the decisive factor in selecting Washington-on-the-Brazos as the site for this momentous occasion was that the town's citizens promised to furnish a suitable meeting place without cost. Noah T. Byars, a South Carolina blacksmith, offered his partially completed building for this historic convention. His offer was eagerly accepted, and it was agreed Byars and his partner, Peter Mercer, would receive $170 for three months' use of the structure, which was to be completed in time for the convention.

The rough cabin was still lacking doors and windows on that cold 33°F March day. Delegates shivered as the wind whistled through the unfinished building. (Noah Byars was not paid his $170.) The war news was as bleak as the weather, and it was not an exultant group of fifty-nine men who gathered in Noah Byars' cabin. Johnson had been defeated at San Patricio, the Alamo was under attack, and its doom was sealed. San Antonio was a mere 140 miles to the west. General Santa Anna could easily send a force and wipe out the convention. In retrospect, you wonder why the Napoleon of the West passed up a great psychological triumph by not capturing these unprotected men in Washington-on-the-Brazos.

There was serious work to be done. The patriots' conference table was nothing but rough planks about forty feet wide with barely enough space for all the men to sit. Buckskin, linen, and broadcloth rubbed shoulders as Richard Ellis from Pecan Point on the Red River presided. Names destined for fame were present: Robert Potter, David Burnet, and Thomas Jefferson Rusk. Also there were four Mexicans loyal to the revolutionists' cause, Lorenzo de Zavala, Jose Antonio Navarro, Francisco Ruiz, and Juan Seguin.

All eyes were on a newcomer to Texas as he rose to present his document at this auspicious meeting. George Campbell Childress had been in Texas less than a month, yet this man from Tennessee would go down in Texas history as the Father of the Declaration of Independence. Childress was dressed in fine black broadcloth with a rich black silk vest and pleated white shirt. His high black boots were polished, and he stood straight as a shingle. Neither slender nor corpulent, the five-foot eleven-inch Tennessean weighed about 180 pounds, and with his high forehead, dark brown hair, and clean-shaven face, the thirty-year-old lawyer created an impressive picture. Childress looked every bit the man who knew how a declaration of independence should be written. In fact, he probably wrote it before he ever arrived at the convention, and it leans heavily on the United States Declaration of Independence.

After describing the state of the Mexican government, the document then listed the grievances the Texans had. Mexico had ceased to protect the lives, liberty, and property of its people. The welfare of Texas was sacrificed for that of Coahuila, which caused the Texans to demand that Texas should be a separate state. There was no public education, no trial by jury, and no freedom of religion. The Mexican government had invaded Texas to carry on a war of extermination, and itself had been the contemptible victim of successive military revolutions, continually exhibiting every characteristic of a weak, corrupt, and tyrannical government. The document ended with a final declaration of independence. Sam Houston strode forward and spoke for the document's acceptance. Within an hour the fifty-nine delegates adopted Childress' masterpiece. Committees were appointed to write a constitution and create an army, design a flag, and all the business of forming a republic. Texas had finally taken an irrevocable step for freedom. There was no turning back. George Childress had done his work well.

Childress was a sensitive man and destined for only that one moment of glory. He had come to Texas because his wife had died and he had felt there was nothing left for him in Tennessee. The young lawyer's uncle was the great empresario, Sterling C. Robertson, and it was from Robertson's colony that Childress attended the convention. After the convention, because of his "high character and enthusiastic patriotism" Childress was appointed as special agent to the United States to seek recognition for the Republic of Texas. The fact that the new Texan was a family friend of Andrew Jackson probably had a lot to do with his appointment as well.

The mission to the United States was a failure, and Childress returned to Nashville and married again. Texas was not grateful to the composer of their Declaration of Independence, because in the next five years, Childress was unable to establish a law practice in his adopted republic.

In 1841 he wrote to President Lamar seeking employment, but was turned down. It was too much for the despondent penniless man.

Childress' sensitive nature and his tendency toward melancholia could not bear the stress of material dependency on friends. It was early in the morning of October 6, 1841 in Galveston that Mrs. Crittendon heard her boarder begging her in piteous terms, "Please, please, oh please, Mrs. Crittendon help me! I must be saved from what I am about to do!" Just as the landlady opened the door, George Childress plunged a bowie knife into his body six times inflicting a mortal wound in his heart. Dr. Ashbel Smith rushed to attend the dying man. Childress' final words were, "I had neither money to bring my wife to this country nor to enable me to visit her." Texas remembered her Father of the Declaration of Independence one hundred years later with a larger-than-life bronze statue at the museum at Washington-on-the-Brazos.

Much had been said about the Texas mystique, and many historians feel the special aura of Texas was created because it was the only state to become a republic before attaining statehood. To forge the Republic, men like Childress, Crockett, Rusk, Sidney Sherman and many more had hardly shaken the dust of the United States from their feet when they were swept up into the tide of the Texas Revolution. Many of these heroic figures died tragically, as Childress, or were forgotten completely, as Sherman. But, without their immeasurable contributions, who knows how the destiny of Texas would have been shaped?

II

The Alamo, Goliad, and the Plains of St. Hyacinth

"To the People of Texas and All Americans in the World..."

Fellow Citizens & Compatriots—I am besieged, by a thousand or more of the Mexicans under Santa Anna—I have sustained a continual Bombardment & cannonade for 24 hours & have not lost a man—The enemy had demanded a surrender at discretion, otherwise, the garrison are to be put to the sword, if the fort is taken— I have answered the demand with a cannon shot, & our flag still waves proudly from the walls—*I shall never surrender or retreat.* Then, I call on you in the name of Liberty, of patriotism & everything dear to the American character, to come to our aid, with all dispatch—The enemy is receiving reinforcements daily & will no doubt increase to three or four thousand in four or five days. If this call is neglected, I am determined to sustain myself as long as possible & die like a soldier who never forgets what is due to his own honor & that of his country—Victory or Death.

**Albert Martin
The Alamo, 1836**

THESE IMMORTAL WORDS STIRRED men's souls. They were written by William Barret Travis on February 24, 1836, and Captain Albert Martin was chosen to deliver Travis' message "To the People of Texas and all Americans in the World." The captain was from Gonzales and knew the country like a book.

The gate flew open! Out into the darkness rode the brave thirty-year-old Texas patriot. Gonzales was seventy miles away. It consisted of one miserable little street of frame buildings, but there was help there for the beleaguered Alamo. Martin had to get the message to all patriotic Texans for his greatly outnumbered comrades. When he reached Gonzales at late afternoon the next day, Martin found young Launcelot Smithers, who would relay the message to San Felipe, ready to ride. Martin hastily penciled a brief note on the back of Travis' impassioned plea:

Since the above was written I have heard a very heavy cannonade during the whole day. I think there must have been an attack made upon the Alamo. We were short of ammunition when I left. Hurry on all the men you can get in haste.

Albert Martin

Albert Martin had served Texas from the very start. When the Mexican Lieutenant Castañeda arrived in Gonzales with his one hundred men on September 29, 1835, to retrieve an old six-pounder cannon, among the armed Texans who taunted him to "come and take it" was Albert Martin. The patriot knew the cannon was safe for he had buried it himself in a peach orchard. The two sides parleyed, as volunteers rushed to the scene. On October 1 the Texans groped their way through a dense fog to the Mexican camp. With them was the cannon, freshly dug up. Suddenly, the fog lifted and the two forces faced each other. More discussions

ensued, and then a rifle went off. Next, the cannon spouted a few nails and horseshoes, and the Mexicans broke and ran. The revolution had begun. (Travis missed this moment of glory, for even great men fall ill. He was in San Felipe with a sore throat.)

When the first Mexican troops arrived at the Alamo on February 22 to begin the siege, Travis sent his emissary to deal with the smooth Colonel Almonte. Under a flag of truce, Captain Albert Martin explained he was speaking for Travis, and that if Almonte wanted to negotiate, Travis would meet him "with much pleasure." Officially, Almonte advised he was not the one to make demands. Unofficially, he hoped the Texans would surrender and promise to never take up arms again and their lives would be spared. Captain Martin returned to his commander. From the walls of the old mission a huge eighteen-pounder cannon belched Travis' reply. As Travis reported to Houston, "I answered them with a cannon shot."

After turning Travis' entreaty for help over to Smithers, Albert Martin scoured the countryside for volunteers to go to the Alamo and face certain death. At two o'clock in the afternoon of February 27 a gallant group of twenty-five men with Albert Martin at their head set out from the square. The next day they picked up seven more willing to sacrifice their lives. On the night of February 29, the "brave 32" from Gonzales rode into the Alamo's walls to die for the freedom of Texas. These men were the only answer to Travis' pleas. They were not from San Felipe or from Fannin at Goliad. The only men who cast their lot with their doomed compatriots were those led by Albert Martin from Gonzales.

Albert Martin was a true lover of the *beau geste,* the gallant gesture. He defied Mexican authority three times, and the third challenge resulted in his death. But, it was such volunteers as Albert Martin that made the Alamo a symbol of Texas freedom.

Historian of the Alamo

**William Physick
Zuber
San Antonio, 1836
(Anderson, 1873)**

THE TINY GARRISON AT the Alamo knew they were doomed. Help was not going to arrive in time, if at all. Santa Anna had ordered his bugler to play the "Deguello," the mournful notes that meant no quarter would be given. The Texans fully understood what it meant. In the quiet evening after the day's battle, it must have been hard on those brave Texans' nerves to hear the ghastly music pierce the darkness. Travis called his men before him and stated what they already knew—there was no hope. Then Travis drew a line with his sword and offered his men the choice of dying gloriously for Texas with him or trying to escape. It makes the fall of the Alamo even more heroic when all men chose to remain except one—Moses Rose.

Rose was actually Louis Rose, a Frenchman who had served in the Napoleonic Wars. A dark swarthy man, Rose spoke the Mexican dialect

Without the historian of the Texas Revolution, William Physick Zuber (left), the world would never have known the saga of how Travis "drew the line" during the siege of the Alamo.

very fluently and could easily pass for one of the enemy. When Rose
elected to leave the defenders of the Alamo, his escape was successful.
Rose wandered back east until he was befriended by the Abraham Zuber
family where he remained several months.

The Zubers had come to Texas in 1830 and built their home in Grimes
County. Their son, William, was away from home with Sam Houston at
San Jacinto. Rose told the Zubers the dramatic story of his narrow escape
and of the final stand Travis had made. The rest of Rose's life is vague
and uneventful. He operated a butcher shop in Nacogdoches and died in
1850 in Louisiana, probably unaware that he would end up in Texas annals as the "Coward of the Alamo."

William Physick Zuber became somewhat of a historian in his later
years and was a charter member of the Texas Historical Commission. He
had fought in the Indian Wars and knew those men destined to shape the
Republic of Texas. Zuber's book, *Eighty Years in Texas,* is a good account of
those post-revolutionary years.

In 1873 the *Quarterly Almanac* published the story of those last days at
the Alamo, and the dramatic story of Travis' last speech to his men was
made known for the first time. Zuber had written Moses Rose's account
of the events and his escape as Rose told it to Zuber's mother, and she in
turn told it to her son.

Zuber's is the only account of Travis' noble gesture. Even Mrs. Dickenson, another of the survivors, never told the story of how Travis drew
the line. (You would think she would remember an event of this magni-
tude.) Here is the story of Travis and his appeal to his men according to
the pen of William Physick Zuber:

Travis lined up the Alamo defenders and began, "My brave companions, our fate
is sealed. Within a very few days, perhaps a very few hours—we must all be in
eternity. This is our destiny, and we cannot avoid it. This is our certain doom . . .
We have no hope for help, for no force that we could ever reasonably have expected,
could cut its way through the strong ranks of these Mexicans. We dare not surrender; for should we do so, that black flag, now waving in our sight, as well as the
merciless character of our enemies, admonishes us of what would be our doom. We
cannot cut our way out through the enemy's ranks; for, in attempting that, we
should all be slain in less than ten minutes. Nothing remains then, but to stay within
this fort, and fight to the last moment . . .

"Then we must die! Our speedy dissolution is a fixed and inevitable fact.—Our
business is, not to make a fruitless effort to save our lives, but to choose the manner
of our death. But three modes are presented to us. Let us choose that by which we
may best serve our country. Shall we surrender, and be deliberately shot, without
taking the life of a single enemy? Shall we try to cut our way out through the Mexican ranks, and be butchered before we can kill twenty of our adversaries? I am opposed to either method; for in either case, we could but lose our lives, without bene-
fiting our friends at home . . . The Mexican army is strong enough to march
through the country, and exterminate its inhabitants, and our countrymen are not
able to oppose them in open field. My choice, then, is to remain in this fort, to resist
every assault, and to sell our lives as dearly as possible.

"Then let us band together as brothers and vow to die together. Let us resolve to
withstand our adversaries to the last; and, at each advance, to kill as many of them
as possible. And when, at last, they shall storm our fortress, let us kill them as they
come! Kill them as they scale our walls! Kill them as they leap within! Kill them as
they raise their weapons, and as they use them! Kill them as they kill our companions! And continue to kill them as long as one of us shall remain alive!

"By this policy, I trust that we shall so weaken our enemies that our countrymen at home can meet them on fair terms, cut them up, expel them from the country, and thus establish their own independence . . . And, *be assured,* our memory will be gratefully cherished by posterity, till all history shall be erased, and all noble deeds shall be forgotten.

"But I leave every man to his own choice. Should any man prefer to surrender, and be tied and shot; or to attempt an escape through the Mexican ranks, and be killed before he can run a hundred yards, he is at liberty to do so.

"My own choice is to stay in this fort and die for my country, fighting as long as breath shall remain in my body. *This I will do, even if you leave me alone.* Do as you think best—but no man can die with me without affording me comfort in the moment of death."

Colonel Travis then drew his sword and with its point traced a line upon the ground extending from the right to the left of the file. Then, resuming his position in front of the center, he said, "I now want every man who is determined to stay here and die with me to come across this line. Who will be the first? March!"

Tapley Holland leaped the line at once exclaiming, "I am ready to die for my country!" His example was followed by every man with the exception of Rose. Every sick man that could walk arose from his bunk and tottered across the line. Colonel Bowie, who could not leave his bed, said, "Boys, I am not able to go to you, but I wish some of you would be so kind as to remove my cot over there." Four men instantly ran to the cot and carried it across the line. Then every sick man that could not walk made the same request and had his cot removed in the same manner.

Artists and writers and Hollywood have immortalized Zuber's thrilling story. Historians tend to be somewhat doubtful of Rose's story, particularly that Rose could remember Travis' long speech as it was actually orated. Zuber also came under fire for waiting thirty-seven years to write about such acts of courage. However, the possibility that such an event could have occurred and perhaps did makes the story of the Alamo all the more exciting. William Physick Zuber has given the fall of the Alamo an even greater mystique and certainly a much more dramatic flair.

Angel of Goliad

Señora Francisca Alvarez Goliad, 1836

THE HEROES OF THE Alamo and Goliad are recalled in the famous battle cries, *Remember the Alamo! Remember Goliad!*, but does anyone remember the Angel of Goliad?

Her name was Francisca Alvarez, and she saved the lives of 20 Texans destined to die on March 27, 1836, when Colonel James W. Fannin and

341 of his men were put to death on orders of General Santa Anna. This hideous day of infamy was the result of incredible indecision on the part of Fannin, a West Point dropout.

Fannin's reason for being at Goliad was his "conviction of its importance as being advantageously located for a depot of reinforcements and military stores. . . ." Fannin was correct in that the Texas occupation of Goliad had contributed more to Cos's defeat in 1835 than the actual siege of San Antonio, for Goliad effectively cut off all supplies from the port of Copano. But, that was 1835, and now Travis was bottled up in the Alamo.

On February 19 Bonham arrived to confer with Fannin. Representing Travis, Bonham presented the idea of moving Fannin's headquarters to San Antonio, but Fannin continued at Goliad keeping his men busy rebuilding the old fort—"Fort Defiance," as Fannin now called it. More than half of his 400 men were recent volunteers from the United States.

On February 25, Travis' impassioned plea for help arrived, but Fannin refused to go, giving no reason. Finally, on February 28, the reluctant colonel made ready to take his men to San Antonio and actually left. However, he turned around and came back, giving that reason that he did not have enough supplies and his method of transport had broken down.

On March 11, Houston reached Gonzales and learned the Alamo had fallen on March 6. The general sent Fannin orders to fall back to Victoria. Burying his guns, Fannin began to retreat, but then he came back and dug them up. He made another fatal mistake by dividing his men into scouting parties which were captured by the Mexican troops with few managing to escape.

On March 18 the enemy cavalry appeared at Fort Defiance, and Fannin planned to retreat that night, but the movement was postponed until the next day. Disregarding Houston's injunction to sink the surplus artillery in the river, Fannin insisted on bringing the nine brass cannons and 500 spare muskets with him. But, he brought no rations for his men.

On a broad unprotected prairie, the colonel halted his men. Had he moved on just a little farther, they would have had water and the protection of trees. The Mexican General Urrea overtook the little band and quickly surrounded the inexperienced 300 with his 1,000 seasoned veterans. It was a long and bloody afternoon, and when darkness fell, nine Texans were dead and fifty-one wounded. Even though many of the men could have escaped, they refused to leave their wounded comrades to the mercy of the Mexicans. The next morning Urrea brought up a twelve-pounder cannon, and Fannin and his men huddled in shallow improvised trenches, helpless against its fire. There was no other recourse except surrender.

It is true that Urrea agreed to spare the lives of the men and offered honorable treatment of the prisoners, but the general had also been present when the murderous decree of December 30, 1835, had been issued by Santa Anna that no prisoners would be taken. Urrea maintained that he felt Santa Anna would honor his agreement with Fannin, as the dictator might hesitate before ordering the death of American citizens.

Santa Anna's chief concern during the entire Revolution was that Texas would receive aid from the United States. When General Jose Antonio Mexia had attacked Tampico in 1835 with three companies of men from New Orleans, one company had broken ranks and was captured by the Mexican forces. Santa Anna waited four weeks, declared the Americans pirates and shot them. New Orleans' reaction was that Mexico was acting within its rights. How badly Santa Anna underestimated U.S. sentiment to his same treatment of the Texans at the Alamo and Goliad.

Urrea wrote to his general the terms of honorable surrender he had offered Fannin. He well knew if his terms had been unconditional, the Texas forces would have fought to the death. In answer to Urrea's letter, Santa Anna ordered immediate death to the "perfidious foreigners." Urrea was not blood-thirsty and had even spared some of Johnson's men at San Patricio and King's men at Refugio. He sent an order to Colonel Jose Nicolas de la Portilla to treat his captives with consideration. But, Portilla received a special order from Santa Anna to "execute the prisoners in his hands at dawn." Portilla may have had moments of reluctance, but there is no doubt as to whose order would be obeyed.

On the day of execution, a Señora Francisca Alvarez, wife of one of the officers under Urrea, arrived. It may be that the lady was actually only one of the camp followers and not actually Alvarez's wife, but regardless of her background, she was smitten with compassion for the doomed men. She found Major William P. Miller left tied for several hours without food and water. She ordered Miller's bonds and those of his men cut and that they be given refreshment. Francisca pleaded so effectively with Lieutenant Colonel Garay that he heeded her pleas and spared twenty of the doctors, interpreters, nurses, and mechanics. Also among those not destined for the field of slaughter was Benjamin Franklin Hughes, the little drummer boy, thanks to the entreaties of this brave woman. Hughes would live to become a prominent Dallas citizen, and he spoke often of the "Angel of Goliad." She concealed several more prisoners upon the parapet of the fort until after the brutal massacre.

The wounded Fannin and forty of his men were murdered in the fort. The rest were taken outside and shot at close range, so most of the soldiers died from the first volley. The rest were run down and bayoneted or lanced as they fled. Still, twenty-eight men somehow managed to reach cover of the wood and escape.

As for the daring Francisca, even on her return to Matamoros, she showed great kindness to the imprisoned Texans there. Later, she was deserted by Alvarez and left penniless. Her final fate is unknown.

Today, Goliad and Fannin's men have their massive memorials to the tragic events that were so fateful in creating the destiny of Texas. But, the "Angel of Goliad" who risked so much for the lives of her enemy has only the briefest of references in Texas history to her heroism.

Survivor of the Fannin Massacre

WILLIAM L. HUNTER WAS shot, had his throat slashed, was stabbed with a bayonet, and finally beaten in the head with a rifle butt, but lived to tell the story of the horror of the massacre of Fannin's men at Goliad.

This incredible survivor of Goliad had recently come to Texas from Virginia as a volunteer with the New Orleans Greys. Hunter was still more American than Texan, but he had irrevocably cast his lot with the floundering Republic.

It was extremely demoralizing to surrender to General Urrea, particularly as few of Fannin's men had ever been in battle before their defeat at Goliad. They had to give up their arms and as prisoners of war be "at the disposal of the Supreme Mexican Government." Urrea assured Fannin that there was no known instance of a prisoner of war who had trusted to the clemency of the Mexican Government being executed. Fannin had no

**William L. Hunter
Goliad, 1836**

choice but to accept the terms and hope that the "disposal" would be parole and return home. Major Juan Jose Holsinger lulled their suspicions with the jovial, "Well, gentlemen, in ten days, home and liberty."

On March 27, 1836, the unwounded Texans were marched from the fort under heavy guard in three divisions. Each division took a separate road from the fort, and the New Orleans Greys were marched along the Victoria road. They must have guessed that death lay waiting for them, even in the midst of the season symbolic of the renewal of life. How very sad it must have been to march toward death along a road replete with the spring wildflowers, particularly for those men who wondered just what noble cause it was they were going to die for.

At selected spots on each of the three roads, the prisoners were halted and their guards turned and fired at point blank range. At the first fire, Hunter was shot in the shoulder. He dropped down and feigned death. But, when the Mexicans began stripping the dead, they found one of the Texans still alive! The Mexican soldier then decided to make certain Hunter would never draw another breath. He slashed the wounded man's throat with a butcher knife, then thrust his bayonet through Hunter's defenseless body a few inches into the ground. As an added cruelty to the Texan, he beat his head with his rifle butt.

A Mr. Fagan, a nearby farmer who was a friend of Mexico, heard the sounds of the massacre. There were heartrending cries of "Don't shoot! For God's sake, don't shoot me!" But, deadly shot after deadly shot followed in quick succession until the last sad cry was hushed in eternal silence.

Fagan went to the scene of the slaughter where the murdered men lay, their bodies left to rot in the sun. He found Colonel Hunter still alive and the man concealed him in a field. Hunter crawled to the river, and after floating down some miles he succeeded in reaching the opposite shore. In six days this amazing man reached Victoria, thirty miles away. He was naked, wounded, famished, and scorched by the sun, but he was alive.

After the revolution William Hunter remained in Texas and was elected to Congress from Refugio County. But, Hunter had not forgotten his inhumane treatment at the hands of the Mexican soldiers. In 1842 when Rafael Vasquez marched on San Antonio, Hunter answered the call to arms. About 1,000 men rallied for the city's aid, but when the Texans arrived, Vasquez had already left.

Hunter spent his remaining years as the chief justice of Goliad County.

Fannin had been foolish not to retreat when he was ordered. The lives of many men would have been saved, but perhaps their death served to further unite Texans in their battle against overwhelming odds. Many historians believe that the Texas mystique was created because it is the only state in the union to have been a republic before it was a state. So, perhaps the cruel massacre of Fannin's men helped add to the special aura of Texas as did the gallant and hopeless stand at the Alamo.

"Remember the Alamo!"

Will you come to the bow'r I have shaded for you?
Our bed shall be roses all sprangled with dew.
And under the bow'r on roses you'll lie
With a blush on your cheek but a smile in your eye.

T O THE TUNE OF a rather suggestive love song rather than a stirring march, Sam Houston's ragtag army attacked the sleeping camp of General Santa Anna. As Samuel Lemsky piped the lilting air of "Come to the Bow'r," 918 Texans moved across the grasslands of the Plain of St. Hyacinth to win what historians consider the sixteenth most important battle in the history of the world.

Commanding the left wing of the Army of the Republic was an officer resplendent in a blue uniform with a close-fitting jacket trimmed with silver lace and a handsome dress sword suspended at his side. Tall, brown-bearded Sidney Sherman was quite a striking contrast from the homespun and woolsey of the rest of the soldiers.

Sherman's company of reckless, drunken, and lawless Kentuckians were real problem children for Houston, but there was no question of their ability to fight. Mrs. Sherman had fashioned her husband's company of volunteers a flag embellished by a rather well-painted figure of a nearly nude Miss Liberty. Sergeant James A. Sylvester, color bearer, affixed a white dress glove to the top of the flagstaff and proudly bore the only flag to fly over the victory on that day of April 21, 1836.

**Lieutenant Colonel
Sidney Sherman
San Jacinto, 1836**

Every Texan remembers the Alamo, but few remember that it was Sidney Sherman who shouted that famous battle cry at San Jacinto.

It was a vengeful Texas army that gathered on the field of battle. They had retreated long enough, and the fact that they were greatly outnumbered meant little. Theirs had been a war of defeat and retreat without a single glorious victory to their credit. Their time was now! Santa Anna would have to pay dearly for his inhuman treatment of Texans.

Suddenly a terrible shout rang forth! *Remember the Alamo! Remember Goliad!* Dashing Sidney Sherman raised his fabled battlecry once again. *Remember the Alamo! Remember Goliad!* Tony Menchaca took up the cry in Spanish and Dick, the black drummer, gave the words a warlike beat. The cry swelled through the ranks of Texans giving added momentum to the attack. In a brief sixteen minutes the Battle of San Jacinto was history. Texas had redeemed her dead heroes of the Alamo and Goliad.

Sherman remained in the Texas he had fought for so well and his flag is now hanging in the House of Representatives in Austin. (Miss Liberty has now been modestly draped.)

Born in 1805 in Massachusetts, this brilliant young officer was orphaned at twelve. Migrating to Kentucky, Sherman was the first man to make cotton bagging by machinery, and in 1835 he sold his successful business to raise a company of fifty-two men to fight for Texas independence.

After the revolution the Colonel organized a successful company to build the Buffalo Bayou, Brazos & Colorado Railroad. During the Civil War this hero of San Jacinto served Texas again as the Commandant of Galveston, and one of many tragedies of his life occurred with the death of his son at the Battle of Galveston. Sherman continued to serve Texas and was elected to the state legislature, but the Colonel's last years were spent in poverty and invalidism.

As so many of those 918 men who had their moment of glory at San Jacinto, Sidney Sherman died forgotten. Only his immortal words have been remembered.

The Horse That Saved Texas

Old Whip
San Jacinto, 1836

THERE HAVE BEEN MANY famous horses throughout history, but the story of the Republic of Texas might have been different if it had not been for "Old Whip." Old Whip served Texas by being headstrong, stubborn, and having a fine homing instinct.

Santa Anna, the "Napoleon of the West," made numerous mistakes that cost him the Battle of San Jacinto. He camped in an open field without cover, he underestimated the tenacity of his foe, and he enjoyed the Mexican custom of a siesta in the middle of enemy territory. Santa Anna's self-confidence was absolutely supreme.

According to the legend, the great womanizer was unable to resist the charms of a mulatto slave girl named Emily Morgan and ordered his troops to take an afternoon rest. The General's tent was set up with its piano and opium cabinet as the great Santa Anna decided to forget the hardships of battle with the lovely Emily (who was later immortalized in the song "The Yellow Rose of Texas").

Santa Anna made one other mistake three days before the battle. He stole a horse. As the Generalissimo was pursuing the retreating Texans he passed William Vince's plantation. Everyone had fled in face of the advancing Mexican Army in the desperate "Runaway Scrape" except Mrs. Brown, a British widow who was not afraid of the Mexicans, and her brash overgrown thirteen-year-old son, Jimmy. Also left behind was Vince's big-boned black half-thoroughbred stallion named Old Whip. Why the horse had not been used as a means of escape remains a mystery, but it was a stroke of good fortune for Texas.

As the Mexicans passed the plantation, Santa Anna spied Old Whip and decided to add him to his numerous other possessions. Jimmy objected, and Colonel Juan Bringas, thinking the lad was much older, hit him with the flat of his saber. Mrs. Brown came running to the aid of her son, screaming at the top of her lungs. When Santa Anna learned the boy was only thirteen, the general apologized for Bringas' action, but he took Old Whip anyway.

Whether Santa Anna ever heard Sidney Sherman's battle cry, "Remember the Alamo! Remember Goliad!" is unknown, but it is known that the element of surprise was most effective for the Texas Army. Realizing his humiliating defeat and knowing he would be made to pay for the Alamo and Goliad, Santa Anna made a hasty escape. He rushed from his elaborate tent, leaped on Old Whip and allowed the powerful horse to take his own course. It must have been a wonderfully comical sight to see the mightly Mexican general galloping pell mell from the field of battle clad only in white silk drawers, a linen shirt with diamond studs, a fine cloth vest with gold buttons, and red morocco slippers, clasping a box of chocolates and a gourd water bottle.

Old Whip's homing instinct was the downfall of His Excellency. The stallion immediately raced back to the corrals near the destroyed bridge on the Vince plantation, and Santa Anna was trapped in the flooding creeks and bayous. Had the fleeing general forced Old Whip to take a more southerly course, there is every possibility he would have reached Filisola's column on the Brazos. The European-trained Filisola would have been back in two days with fresh troops to take on the Texans to his advantage, and the fate of Texas might have been much different.

There are many ironic quirks that decide the fate of men, and Santa Anna's greed for a fine horse resulted in his defeat. Lost in the high grass, the Texas foe was captured and gave the Republic the trump card in their dangerous game. As for Old Whip, he spend the rest of his years as one of the most popular studs in Texas. There were a lot of people who wanted a colt from the horse that captured Santa Anna.

The Capture of the Hero of Tampico

You will find the Hero of Tampico, if you find him at all, retreating on all fours in high grass. And, he will be dressed as badly at least as a common soldier. Examine every man you find very closely.

General Sam Houston

**James A. Sylvester
San Jacinto, 1836**

THE BATTLE WAS OVER. Prisoners were taken. The dead were strewn grotesquely over the plains of San Jacinto. Texas had won despite overwhelming odds, but the arch enemy, Santa Anna, had escaped.

No one knew how the wily Mexican general had managed to evade capture, but he was not among the prisoners. Heeding Houston's wise advice, patrols searched the bayous and flooding fields for their prize. What was victory if the hated Santa Anna was able to reach reinforcements and retaliate with fresh troops? He had to be found!

A sharp-eyed Kentuckian, James A. Sylvester, captured a Mexican in a dirty hide hat, never dreaming his prize was Santa Anna.

After the stolen horse, Old Whip, had raced back to his corral at the Vince plantation with El Presidente, the stallion halted and Santa Anna dismounted. Old Whip trotted off, reins dragging, to become the most famous horse in Texas. Crouching and hiding in the tall grass, His Excellency managed to find his way to the abandoned slave quarters where he found some rags that had been left behind. Santa Anna may have had the reputation of being brilliant, but you wonder why he disguised himself so poorly. He discarded his fine vest, but he kept on the beautiful linen shirt and red morocco shoes that he had on when he fled from the arms of the slave girl, Emily Morgan. How incongruous these rich clothes must have looked with his filthy rags.

Fortunately for Texas, the greatest Mexican general did not have the greatest sense of direction. Instead of turning toward General Filisola's reinforcements, Santa Anna headed back toward the Texas camp. And, as his bad luck would have it, one of Colonel Burleson's patrols happened by. They were Sion Bostick, Alfred Miles, Charles Thompson, Joseph Vermillion, Joel Robinson, and James Sylvester. Sylvester was the color bearer for Sidney Sherman's Kentucky volunteers who had carried the only flag at the Battle of San Jacinto.

The sharp-eyed Sylvester spotted some buck deer almost hidden by the dense grass and saw the chance for fresh meat. Just as the Kentucky sharpshooter drew a bead on the largest buck, a movement in the grass frightened the deer away. Curious as to the cause of the deer's flight, Sylvester turned his horse toward the wavering grass. He flushed a Mexican in a dirty hide hat who tried to run but fell flat on his face. Sylvester yelled to the rest of the men, "Hey, I've got me a prisoner!" Little did the Texas soldier realize what a prize he had captured.

Bostick and Sylvester kicked the Mexican to his feet and searched him. Bostick wanted to shoot him, but Sylvester wanted the prisoner alive. (Bostick would be the first of many who wanted Santa Anna dead.) The rest of the Texans rode up to view their captive, and as only Joel Robinson could speak Spanish, he began to question the Mexican. The grateful prisoner was so overjoyed to find someone who spoke his language, he began to kiss Robinson's hand.

Noting the Mexican's fine shirt and diamond studs, Robinson asked him where Santa Anna and General Cos had gone. Receiving no answer, the Texans decided to take their unusual trophy back to General Houston. Driving him in front of their horses like a cow, the great Generalissimo complained and moaned bitterly. How degrading for The Napoleon of the West! In answer, Miles pushed him forward with the tip of his lance. Santa Anna begged and pleaded to be given a ride and kept kissing Miles' hand. Miles became disgusted and said, "I'm sick of this. I'm going to kill him." Robinson then took pity on the cringing, whining Mexican and put him behind him on his horse. As they rode back to the Texas lines, the prisoner kept asking Robinson questions about the battle and was surprised to find the Texans only numbered about 900 men. Imagine the surprise of Sylvester and his group when they rode into camp and the Mexican prisoners began chanting, "El Presidente! El Presidente!" Santa Anna was betrayed by his own men.

During those days of Houston's retreat, Santa Anna had sent insulting letters to Houston accusing him of cowardice and gloating over the Texas defeats. Don't you know Santa Anna regretted all those nasty notes now. Houston had been quite badly wounded in the ankle and was resting under a tree. The little party deposited their marvelous gift, and with outrageous aplomb Santa Anna introduced himself, "I am Antonio Lopez de Santa Anna, President of Mexico, Commander-in-chief of the Army, and I put myself at the disposition of the brave General Houston. I wish to be treated as a general should when a prisoner of war." With that the arrogant Mexican sat on a box and proceeded to take his opium.

Sylvester did not return to Kentucky. He was a member of the Somervell Expedition in 1842, but he left Texas the next year for New Orleans. A printer by trade, Sylvester swapped 640 acres in what is now the heart of Dallas for a mangy mule and rode off to a job on the *New Orleans Picayune*. Among Sylvester's papers in Galveston's Rosenberg Library is the following manuscript along with his promotion to captain:

Presented
to
James A. Sylvester
by
General Sam Houston

as a tribute of regard for his *gallant* and *vigilant* conduct first in the battle of San Jacinto and subsequently in the capture of Santa Anna, whose thanks were tendered by Santa Anna, in my presence to Captain Sylvester, for his generous conduct towards him, when captured.

Sam Houston
San Augustine 3rd Aug. 1836

The Runaway Scrape

The owls were singing a funeral dirge and wolves and buzzards were waiting to bury us.

**Dilue Rose Harris
Columbus, 1836**

DILUE ROSE ALWAYS DID have a way with words. In another place, another time, she probably would have become a famous writer. But women on the Texas frontier were too busy just staying alive to indulge in frivolities. It was in her later years that Dilue would write a slim little book that would supply historians with a first hand view of those heroic days of the revolution, *The Reminiscences of Mrs. Dilue Rose Harris.*

The Rose family immigrated to Texas in 1833 when their daughter, Dilue, was eight years old. She never forgot their trip to their new home on the Brazos River about fifteen miles from Harrisburg. Years later she would recall her fears when the owls sang their funeral dirge. Fortunately for students of Texas history, Dilue also never forgot the nightmare events of the Runaway Scrape.

It was planting time in February of 1836. The news had arrived that General Santa Anna and his brother-in-law General Cos were marching with their great armies into Texas. There was some concern, but no one worried too much those February days, for the Commander-in-Chief, Sam Houston, would take care of those Mexicans. Then Colonel Travis' impassioned plea for aid to the besieged Alamo arrived, and all the men rushed to join Houston's Army of the Republic.

Times were tense and frightening. It was feared that those left behind would have to flee to the United States. What would happen to their homes in the path of retreating Texas soldiers and advancing Mexican armies? Clothing, bedding, and furniture were hidden in the woods and precious heirlooms were buried. It was hoped they would still be in their hiding places when Texas won her independence. Meanwhile, the young Dilue was busy "melting lead in a pot, dipping it with a spoon and molding bullets."

Then came the dreadful news. The Alamo had fallen. Fannin and his men had been massacred at Goliad. It was time to run for their lives, and it couldn't have been a worse time. The Trinity River was at flood, the weather was freezing, and there was no bridge. The Rose family suffered as did many others with the death of one of their daughters. Dilue remembered so vividly:

Our hardships began at the Trinity. The river was rising and there was a struggle to see who should cross first. Measles, sore eyes, whooping cough, and every other disease that man, woman, or child is heir to, broke out among us. Our party now consisted of the five white families I first mentioned, and Mr. Adam Stafford's Negroes. We had separated from Mrs. M——. and other friends at Vince's bridge. The horrors of crossing the Trinity are beyond my power to describe. One of my little

sisters was very sick, and the ferryman said that those families that had sick children should cross first. When our party got to the boat the water broke over the banks above where we were and ran around us. We were several hours surrounded by water. Our family was the last to get to the boat. We left more than five hundred people on the west bank. Drift wood covered the water as far as we could see. The sick child was in convulsions. It required eight men to manage the boat.

When the refugees felt they could go no farther, the glorious news came that Houston had defeated Santa Anna at San Jacinto. They could return to their homes. The bedraggled and miserable Texans began their long trek back to their homes, praying there was still a home left.

The Phantoms of Orozimbo

Dr. and Mrs. James Aeneas Phelps West Columbia, 1836

THERE IS NOTHING LEFT now except the famous oak tree, and even that is not easy to find. But, here in 1836 underneath its huge branches stood the gracious and lovely plantation home of Dr. James Aeneas E. Phelps—Orozimbo. The Phelpses were one of Stephen F. Austin's original 300 colonists, and Dr. Phelps served Texas

The mansion is gone, but the massive oaks remain at Orozimbo Plantation, Santa Anna's Texas prison.

well at the Battle of San Jacinto. Orozimbo hosted many famous Texans, but perhaps the most famous, or infamous as the case may be, was none other than General Santa Anna.

Capturing the hated Mexican leader was one thing, but deciding what to do with him was something else. Many, many Texans wanted Santa Anna dead, but Sam Houston wisely determined to save his adversary. Santa Anna was worth much more alive. Not only would he prove the generosity of Texans, but El Presidente would grant more favorable peace terms than the Mexican government. Also, Houston wanted a personal witness to the events at San Jacinto.

Shortly after the battle Houston negotiated the Treaty of Velasco with the dictator. In the treaty were secret clauses that the boundary would be the Rio Grande and Santa Anna would be sent home in safety to work for ratification of the treaty and recognition of the Texas Republic. There was a large faction in Texas who wanted to take all of Mexico as well as to execute Santa Anna.

Velasco was not the place to keep the Generalisimo a prisoner. He was too vulnerable to assassination or escape, so he was removed for a brief period to the Patton plantation not far from West Columbia. It was during this time that the incident of the beautiful Spanish lady and the dropped glove occurred. According to the *History of Brazoria County* a very beautiful Spanish lady came to visit her countryman bringing dainty edibles and fine wine. After an animated conversation with the "Napoleon of the West," she rose to go and let her glove fall at the general's feet. Major Patton, who had been in attendance, recovered the glove and returned it to the lady. Again the glove fell. This time the wary Major discovered a note written on thin paper in one of the fingers. The lovely lady had supplied Santa Anna with drugged wine for his guards and a note that horses would be kept waiting for his escape. If this plan failed, another bottle marked a certain way contained poison. Somehow, Santa Anna drank the poisoned wine, but Major Patton drove him immediately to Orozimbo where Dr. Phelps saved his life.

Finally, Santa Anna was taken under heavy guard to a very genteel prison at the fairly isolated Phelps' plantation. From July to November of 1836 Santa Anna remained at Orozimbo closely guarded by twenty of Houston's most trusted men.

A wonderful ghost story is told about Santa Anna's term of sanctuary at Orozimbo. If the remote plantation was a good prison, it could also lend itself to easy escape. It seems that a bold Mexican officer had a plan for his general's daring rescue. On a dreary rainy night the conspirators arrived to overpower the unsuspecting guards and take Santa Anna back to Mexico.

As the would-be rescuers neared the grounds of Orozimbo the unearthly frantic cries of wild and ferocious hounds were heard. As though in the heat of the chase, the dogs' eerie yelps and barks awakened the Phelps' household. Santa Anna's escape plans were foiled.

But where had the guardian hounds whose warning had been so needful come from? Orozimbo had no dogs, nor were there any in those empty forests. Some say the mastifs belonged to a brave man who died at Goliad. When he left to fight for independence, his dogs had refused to eat and had wandered away to roam wild. But the dog's owner had lived

at Washington-on-the Brazos. Had his hounds really roamed those many miles?

The hounds of Orozimbo add to the aura of mystery that surrounds Santa Anna's imprisonment.

Later, another atempt was made on Santa Anna's life by a Texas soldier. Once again the Phelps' came to their prisoner's rescue. Mrs. Phelps threw her arms around Santa Anna and prevented the soldier from firing.

There are many stories about the Mexican dictator's confinement and some seem a bit far-fetched, but there is no doubt that Santa Anna was later to repay the Phelps with the greatest gift of all, the life of their son.

Orlando Phelps was a member of the ill-fated Mier Expedition in 1843. When Santa Anna received word of his special prisoner, the dictator had young Phelps brought to the presidential palace, gave him $500 in gold and had him sent back to Texas.

In spite of the continued animosity between Texas and Mexico, Santa Anna regularly sent presents to the Phelps family at Christmastime, usually fine bedspreads. The general who could easily order no quarter given at the Alamo and the immediate massacre of Fannin at Goliad never forgot his honorable treatment at Orozimbo.

III
A Republic United,
A State Divided

Financier of the Revolution

Samuel May
Williams
Galveston, 1836

I N WARTIME, IT IS a rare hero indeed that emerges other than on the battlefield, and Sam Williams was not at Goliad with Fannin nor at the Alamo with Travis, and he was never part of Houston's army during his moments of glory at the Battle of San Jacinto. But, without Sam Williams there would have been no Republic, for it was this true patriot of Texas that arranged for the financing of the revolution. Also, even though the Texas Navy never ruled the seas, without Sam Williams there might have been no Texas Navy at all. Williams' contribution to Texas was in financing the Republic's heroic deeds.

When all is said and done, wars and republics have to have money, and even the most dedicated of firebrand heroes have to pay their bills someday. To make the revolution possible and the Republic survive, it took a lot of money—money that an eternally bankrupt Texas did not have. Somehow Sam Williams was able to convince bankers in the East to believe in Texas.

When Sam Williams came to Texas in 1823 he was twenty-eight years old, and ready for adventure and success in a new land. Williams had spent a short time as private secretary to Andrew Jackson, and Stephen F. Austin had induced the brilliant youth to come with him to Texas. Austin was unable to get his first colony organized until 1824, but Sam Williams was willing to wait. Texas was an exciting challenge, and opportunities were unlimited. Having become fluent in Spanish and French as a clerk in New Orleans, the young bookkeeper became employed as an interpreter to pass the time until Austin arrived to take charge.

In 1824 Williams became the official secretary of Austin's colony and took over the Public Land Office at San Felipe de Austin. For eleven years Sam Williams was Austin's confidential and indispensable assistant. Many a Texan had cause to be grateful for the meticulous records this dedicated and hard-working secretary kept of deeds and certificates of title.

Supplies were so scarce in the struggling colony that no suitable book for a register was available. Williams sent to his brother in New Orleans for such a book and then had to dispatch a man on a mule to bring it from Natchitoches, Louisiana. All of this effort took six months just to get the prized book to San Felipe, but without Sam Williams' detailed records, many Texans would have lost title to their land.

Williams' compensation for his work was always inadequate. Not only did he have his clerical duties so necessary to the land grants, but Austin left him in charge of the colony's affairs when he had to leave San Felipe. In addition, the secretary had to take special care of Austin's house.

Sam Williams never fought on the battlefield, but he remains one of the true heroes of the Republic of Texas. His Galveston home is now a public shrine.

"Keep the crib and smoke house locked . . . and care for my two motherless pigs," Austin admonished. The great empresario did repay his dutiful secretary with the commodity most plentiful—land.

With all of his responsibilities, Sam Williams still had time to fall in love, and in 1828 he married Sarah Scott. Their marriage was one of great congeniality and affection. Nine children were born to the Williams and five survived. In his later years Williams became somewhat embittered over his career, but his family never failed to give him a great deal of satisfaction. His wife was plagued with failing eyesight, but her adoring husband wrote her letters with "words as big as sparrows," to compensate.

In 1835, the year before the Revolution, the legislature of Coahuila and Texas feared Santa Anna's rise to power and sold off public lands for defense. Individuals in Texas could buy 400 leagues (about two million acres) for 47 cents an acre. Milam, Bowie, and Sam Williams invested in this bonanza. But, land speculation was abhorrent to Austin, and it also roused great resentment among the colonists. In November of 1836 Austin wrote his secretary, ". . . you have wounded me very deeply, but you are so rooted in my affections that, with all your faults, you are at heart too much like a wild heedless brother to be entirely banished." Austin died less than two months later.

The year before his venture into land speculation Williams had entered into a partnership with Thomas F. McKinney and founded the maritime commerce in Texas. Operating out of Galveston with three small steam vessels, the firm was extremely successful. So staunch was McKinney & Williams in supporting the Revolution, it was to them the Republic looked for finances.

Even though Sam Williams had joined with Austin in his initial fidelity to Mexico, events pulled him closer and closer toward the Revolution. By 1835 there was a price on his head by the Mexican government.

Williams was in the East when the Revolution began, but when he returned to Texas with him were 700 volunteers, a fleet of 3 vessels and a schooner loaded with provisions and arms which he had secured by becoming personally responsible for the payment. The financier had many connections in the East and spent two years working for the Republic at McKinney & Williams' expense. It was years before the firm was recompensed for their expenses. Finally, in 1856 $40,000 was voted to McKinney & Williams in the face of great hostility on the part of the legislature. What short memories they had! After twenty years, the firm's great service to Texas was forgotten.

With the inauguration of Lamar, Williams was replaced as loan commissioner, but he was still the naval agent for the Republic and met with great success. In June of 1839, the *Viper*, the vanguard of the second Texas Navy sailed into Galveston manned by five sailors and carrying Dr. Anson Jones, Moses Austin Bryan, and Samuel May Williams.

The career of this incredible man was far from over. McKinney & Williams began to invest in the fledgling city of Galveston. The firm began in international maritime commerce, and became a decisive factor in the economic development of Galveston and Texas. The next step was to have a bank worthy of this growing little city.

Anti-banking sentiment was so strong in Texas no legislature would authorize a charter. Many of the Texas pioneers had lost money in bank panics before coming to Texas, and so had no use for banks. In spite of extreme opposition, in 1841 the Texas government allowed Williams to issue $30,000 in paper money. It caused a scandal in the government, and Sam Houston was accused of being bribed. However, Sam Houston was used to accusations and realized a bank was necessary.

The Commercial and Agricultural Bank opened its doors in Galveston on December 30, 1847, but 1848 was not a good year. Prosecuted and persecuted by anti-banking factions, Williams' last project seems to have engendered more vexation, anxieties, and bitterness than any other experience in his years of service to Texas. When the "Father of Texas Banking" died in 1858, his physician diagnosed the case as "assuming the features of no disease in particular, but seeming rather to be a general debility—a giving way mentally and physically." It seems the man who gave so much of his life, his time, and his personal funds to Texas could no longer stand up to the "slings and arrows of outrageous fortune." Sam's beloved Sarah soon followed her devoted husband, and they are both buried in the Episcopal cemetery in the city they helped to build.

Now, a grateful Galveston Historical Foundation has restored the Williams' home at 3601 Avenue P, and it is open for tours. The original furnishings are there, including the piano in the parlor said to have been thrown overboard from a ship that ran aground near Galveston. Near the piano is the reclining chair that a loving father sat in and listened to his little Caddy's recitals. This financial genius becomes a real living personality as recorded hidden voices recite vignettes in his homelife. One voice reveals the sentiments of this forgotten hero, "So much time has passed. I just turned my head for a moment, and they were all grown . . . can you tell me where all the years have gone?" The years went by with Sam Williams serving his Republic, his state, and his nation.

His Weapon—His Jerusalem Blade

WILDCAT MORRELL SPENT THE first nineteen years of his life a true sinner. He gambled on the horses, drank his share of hard liquor, and generally raised hell. Then one fateful day in 1822 this hard-living young man was plowing a field and the Lord spoke to "Wildcat." After this overpowering Spiritual revelation Z. N. Morrell became a dedicated man of God.

By the time he was twenty Morrell was married and a Baptist preacher. "Wildcat" attacked the ministry with the same zeal and ardor he had given his sinful life, and the Lord was the winner.

For fourteen years in South Carolina and Tennessee Morrell made the ministry a fulltime calling. He gave himself without reserve, averaging a sermon a day. He almost gave the ministry his life as well, for this excessive labor resulted in hemorrhaging lungs. The preacher was ordered to cease the ministry and seek a warmer climate.

Z. N. Morrell
Marlin, 1842

Reverend Z. N. Morrell, better known as "Wildcat," roared across the Texas frontier with a special kind of weapon—his Bible, which he called his Jerusalem Blade.

Morrell gave Texas a great deal of thought, but since Catholicism held sway, the devoted Baptist pastor decided to "wait with patience until further light." With his wife and four children Morrell moved to Mississippi, where, in spite of bleeding lungs, he founded three Baptist churches.

After one particularly busy Sunday in December of 1835 Morrell returned home in a cold drizzling rain to find a group of old friends from Tennessee waiting for him. "Texas fever" assailed Morrell. Two days later the tubercular preacher was astride his mule on the way to Texas. Brother Morrell traveled, preached the gospel, organized churches, and held revivals for about $250 a year. Often his horses alone cost $300 a year. Z. N. Morrell did not come to Texas to get rich.

The Mexican invasion of 1842 brought great excitement, and Brother Morrell—though a cripple—was right there in the midst of the action. A small band of thirteen men under Captain Jack Hays kept watch near San Antonio with nothing to eat but cold flour. Mutiny arose in the camp and Captain Hays asked Brother Morrell to speak. He mounted his horse, rode out in front of the group and with as cheerful a face as possible addressed them: "Boys, when I left Colonel Caldwell's camp, I felt like I was forty years old. When I had starved one day, I felt like I was thirty-five. After that, on two spoonfuls a day I felt like I was twenty-five, and this morning, when our cold flour and coffee are both out, I feel like I was only twenty-one years old and ready for action." Tempers cooled and order was restored.

When Brother Morrell learned of Captain Dawson's defeat and the slaughter of his men, he feared his son was among those killed. With three volunteers the minister rode to the scene of the battle. "The body of my son could not be found. The place was so horrible that two of the men with me rode away." Morrell's son was among the prisoners taken from San Antonio when the Mexican army evacuated the town.

A council of war was held and General Mayfield gave a gloomy harangue and urged the pursuit be abandoned. Morrell was furious. His son was among those helpless prisoners. Long years afterward Brother Morrell wrote: "Heaven I hope has forgiven me for the animosity I felt towards the man."

With his son in chains, his wife's health rapidly declining, and the death of a beloved elder daughter, such a cloud of sorrow hung over Morrell's memories of 1843 that he left it to others to record. "I can't write them," the man of God lamented.

When his son returned home, Brother Morrell resumed his pastoral work. "I buckled on my armor to fight His battles while I still lived." "Wildcat" never took his armor off again. At eighty, Brother Morrell went to the arms of the God he had talked about all of his adult life. On his simple marker were the words, "A sinner saved by grace." Brother Morrell was known to use his rifle when circumstances required it, but his real weapon for settling the Texas frontier was his "Jerusalem blade," as he called his Bible.

Texans Have Long Memories

HIGH ON A HILL overlooking the old town of La Grange is a monument to one of the saddest and most macabre events in Texas' long struggle with Mexico—the Black Bean Incident.

In 1842 the young Texas Republic was struggling with its endless problems, including the fact that Mexico had never agreed to the terms of surrender after the battle of San Jacinto. Mexican attacks continued, and when a force under the Dutch General Adrian Woll captured San Antonio, President Sam Houston was forced to take action.

The command to pursue Woll was given to a colorless and safe leader, Alexander Somervell, who would do nothing rash. Unfortunately, most of the Texas volunteers were freebooters only interested in plunder. When the Texans reached Laredo, they looted and pillaged the town. Somervell did all the right things. He arrested the rabble, returned stolen property, and refused to cross the Rio Grande. The men promptly deserted except for 300 diehards who elected Colonel William Fisher as their commander.

Walter Paye Lane
La Grange, 1848

Fisher attacked Mier on December 23, 1842, and secured the town; however, Fisher was wounded. When a Mexican force under General Pedro Ampudia arrived, the Texans voted to surrender. The usual promises were made that the Texans' lives would be spared, and they would be marched to Mexico City. En route to the Capital, the Texans escaped, but 182 were recaptured. Ewen Cameron who masterminded the escape, was among those doomed prisoners.

Santa Anna was enraged and demanded all the Texans be executed. Britain and the United States intervened, so Santa Anna agreed to one death in ten. A local official at Saltillo devised the lottery of the beans. There would be 159 white beans and 17 black, thus "democratically" deciding who would be executed. The following description from a survivor of the Mier expedition is from the Houston *Telegraph and Register,* May 1845.

So entirely unexpected was this murderous announcement, so atrocious in its character so inhuman and indecent in the haste of its consummation, that a stupor seemed to pervade, not a word escaping the lips of any for more than a minute. While we were marshalled in an extended line, a Mexican subaltern and soldier entered the yard together, bearing a bench, and an earthen crock. A handkerchief was folded as to hide the color of the beans and thrown over the crock, and a list of our names placed in the hands of the interpreter. When these funeral preliminaries had been completed, the name of our dauntless leader was first called, who, with a step as stately and brow as serene as he had ever previously worn, stepped forward and drew.

Each man in his order on the list continued to be called until the seventeen black beans had been taken from the pot. When a bean was drawn it was handed to an officer, and the jar well shaken before the dread lottery proceeded. In many instances the doomed victim was forced to return to the fatal urn to allow the comrade to whom he was chained to try the issue of life and death. Not a step faltered, not a nerve shook, as the sickening ceremony went on. Several of the Mexican officers seemed deeply affected, shedding tears and turning their backs. Others leaned forward over the crock as though they had heavy wagers on the result. Three-fourths of the beans were exhausted before the fatal seventeen had been drawn.

As twilight advanced two files of infantry of twenty men each and the whole body of cavalry escorted the doomed men to the eastern wall. Here being made to kneel down with their backs to their butchers, they were blindfolded and shot in two parties successively, nine first and eight afterward. The surviving prisoners were forced to remain silent or be shot while the execution was in progress. Tears forced their way down many a rugged cheek as silent and manacled we listened to the mournful notes of the dead march. The wall against which the doomed men were placed was so near us we could distinctly hear every order, the prayers of the kneeling men, the clank of the muskets brought up to aim—the sharp burst of the discharge mingled with shrill cries of anguish and heavy groans, as body and soul took their sudden and bloody leave.

Ewen Cameron had drawn a white bean, but General Antonio Canales, the Commander at Mier, had personally seen to Cameron's execution anyway. Houston was powerless to retaliate, but the Texans have long memories. For six years the bones of this ghastly human lottery lay rotting in their common grave. But during the Mexican War they were recovered by a brave scout named Walter Lane.

There were two roads to San Louis Potosi—one by Matchuala, a large town, the other by the great hacienda of Salado where the seventeen Texas Mier prisoners had drawn the black beans and died. The two roads were divided by a large range of mountains. While on a scouting mission, Lane took the left hand road and actually entered the city of Matchuala with its 20,000 people and a garrison of several hundred men. He ordered and obtained dinner at a hotel, announced that a large American army was nearby, and then remounting, retired across the mountain to the other road and struck the hacienda of Salado. Seizing the alcalde, he ordered the resurrection of the bones of the seventeen martyred Texans. Then he demanded mules, packs, saddles, and all things necessary to bear them away. Lane tipped his hat to the alcalde and the assembled villagers and bore the relics to General Taylor's headquarters.

The bones were conveyed to La Grange, as Cameron had been from there. With all solemnity, in the presence of thousands, the Black Bean victims were interred on Monument Hill. Few Texans know that to Walter P. Lane Texas is indebted for the possession of these mementos of heroism.

Walter Lane was born in Ireland in 1817, and as so many Texas soldiers he was a volunteer from the United States a brief few weeks before San Jacinto. Lane fought so bravely at San Jacinto he was promoted to second lieutenant and saved from death by the quick action of Mirabeau Lamar when a Mexican lance pierced his shoulder.

Following the Revolution Lane joined a survey party in Navarro County. If there was one thing the Indians realized early in the settling of the west, once a survey group arrived on their hunting grounds, the wagon trains were not far behind. Lane's party of twenty-two men were surrounded by Indians and all but three of the comrades were slain. Somehow Lane survived the "Surveyors Fight" by crawling out of range to safety in spite of a badly shattered leg.

After his heroic recovery of the victims of Mier, Lane ended the Mexican War as a major. During the Civil War Lane had eight horses shot out from under him at the Battle of Corinth, and he was wounded at the Battle of Mansfield. When this dedicated Texas soldier died in 1892, he was buried with full military honors, truly deserving his title as Texas' "Fighting Irishman."

The Great Hanging

D URING THE CIVIL WAR Texas distinguished herself nobly with Hood's Brigade and Terry's Rangers. Dick Dowling's stand at Sabine Pass was one of the Confederacy's overwhelming victories. However, as the war tore the nation apart, in the South there were still many citizens whose loyalties lay with the Union.

**Thomas Barrett
Gainesville, 1862**

Dr. Thomas Barrett cast
the only dissenting vote
on a jury that sentenced
40 men to hang for dis-
loyalty to the South dur-
ing the Civil War.

Up in the north and northwestern part of Texas eight counties had cast
majorities against the Ordinance of Secession by which Texas withdrew
from the Union. It was the west that owned no cotton fields and were
non-slave counties. Old Texas was in the East, new Texas was the West
and they wanted no part of the Confederacy.

There was bound to be trouble in those recalcitrant counties, and in
October of 1862 Brigadier General William Hudson, C.S.A., learned of
a Unionist underground operating in and around his district. Hudson
conferred with his staff and designed a plan by which they might obtain
the secret schemes of the conspirators. The Confederates were lucky and
penetrated the "Peace Party Conspiracy" in spite of its secret signs, grip,
and password. Armed troops carried out raids in Cooke County and took
seventy men into custody.

On the same day as the arrest, Colonel William C. Young of the 11th
Texas Cavalry named a committee of five which in turn recommended
twelve citizens for a "citizens court." This court was instructed to examine all crimes and offenses committed, determine the innocence or guilt
of the accused and pronounce appropriate punishment.

Serving on the jury was Thomas Barrett. Barrett had arrived in
Gainesville in 1860 with his second wife and thirteen children. Not only
did he practice medicine, Barrett was an ordained minister in the Disci-
ples of Christ Church. The Citizens Court tried the seventy men and
found thirty-nine of the Peace Party members guilty of conspiracy and
insurrection and also guilty of disloyalty and treason against Texas and
the Confederacy. Three other men who were in the Confederate army

were court martialed and found guilty of the same crimes. The sentence was death by hanging. Only one member of the jury was opposed to the sentence, Thomas Barrett. Barrett's opposition meant nothing. There was such violent anti-Union sentiment that all forty-two conspirators were hanged in one grisly day.

Not much is known about this brave man who dared to voice his beliefs against overwhelming odds, but Thomas Barrett's act of courage caused him to have to flee for his life. First Barrett moved to Vernon and then to Bell County, but when the war was was over Reconstruction courts prosecuted the jury members. To save his life, Barrett had to flee again, this time to Tennessee.

Barrett did return to Gainesville and was finally tried and cleared of all charges against him. In 1885 Barrett published "The Great Hanging at Gainesville, Cooke County, Texas, October A.D. 1862," which has become an extremely rare piece of Texana. A companion piece was written by George Washington Diamond, a Henderson, Texas, publisher, but it remained unpublished until 1963. There are still many mysteries and conjectures about "The Great Hanging." One thing is certain, "The Great Hanging" is a black mark on the history of Texas. Only Thomas Barrett dared make a stand against this terrible injustice.

"Treue der Union"

T HE BATTLE OF THE NUECES, August 10, 1862—what a tragic day in Texas history! German immigrants to Texas were caught up in a contest of wills between the North and the South. Germany had no slaves, no blacks, and not enough time had elapsed for them to become Texans rather than Europeans. Only one concept was clear, slavery lessened the value of their own labor, so they would remain "true to the Union."

When the German settlers of Kerr, Kendall, and Gillespie counties formed the Union Loyal League, the Confederacy declared those counties to be in open rebellion and subject to martial law. Wisely, the Union Loyal League decided to disband. All Germans who still wanted to join the Union met at Turtle Creek in Kerr County on August 1, 1862, and rode for Mexico.

Of the sixty-eight men who gathered, many were from the small German community of Comfort. Even though they were heavily armed, the Germans turned their exodus from Texas into a holiday. With songs and jokes, the band headed south. About twenty miles from Bracketville the

**Wilhelmine Stieler
Comfort, 1862**

A simple stone obelisk engraved "Treue der Union" in tiny Comfort is the only Union monument in the South.

Union loyalists camped unaware they were being pursued by the Confederate troops.

Just before dawn the "battle" occurred. Rebel forces, ninety-four strong, attacked. The Germans were so taken by surprise, there was no time to defend themselves, and nineteen were killed outright. Nine were captured and then shot, but somehow forty escaped. Among those captured and murdered at the Nueces were sixteen-year-old Henry Stieler and eighteen-year-old Theodor Bruckisch. They were too young to die, but tragic incidents brought their brief lives to an end.

Stieler had escaped from the Nueces battleground, but later fell into the hands of the Confederates. The clever lad managed to convince the leaders that he was actually on his way to join the Southern cause but had lost his way. Unfortunately for both boys, just at this time Bruckisch was brought in. Not being as quick-witted as Stieler, Bruckisch instantly betrayed himself and Stieler as well. Both boys were shot immediately and their bodies left unburied where they fell as were those of all the men slain that day.

When the news of the murders reached the Stieler home, a brave young sister, Wilhelmine, declared that the body of her brother should not be left lying unburied and exposed to the prey of buzzards and wild animals. As no man dared jeopardize his life to help her, Wilhelmine and her mother went alone to the scene of the massacre.

The two courageous women defiantly passed through the ranks of Confederates with such courage, the soldiers did not prevent them from carrying out the burial. The heartbroken mother became deranged with grief and the task remained to Wilhelmine.

When the determined girl found she was not strong enough to dig the grave, she covered her brother's body with brush and weighted it down with rocks so the wild animals could not tear away the cover. After protecting Bruckisch's body also, the exhausted mother and daughter returned home. In the course of time, Wilhelmine returned to bring the remains of her beloved brother home to the family farm. To add to the tragedy, her mother never regained her sanity.

On August 20, 1865, E. Degener, the father of two of the victims of the Nueces and twenty-five men went to the battlefield to recover and bury the remains of their friends. A funeral procession of 300 mourners was led by the fathers of the victims under the Union banner "Martyrs of Loyalty."

The next year on the day of the infamous battle a plain white obelisk was erected in the memory of those slain with the simple epitaph "Treue der Union" (Loyalty to the Union). It is the only monument to the Northern cause in the South.

IV
Of Cowboys and Indians

A Better Man Than His Murderers

**Chief Bowles
Tyler, 1839**

S AM HOUSTON WAS LIVID with anger! His work, his treaty, his friendship with the Cherokee Indians were all in vain! Texas had destroyed one of its greatest allies in its greed for the Indians' rich land. During the Battle of the Neches, not only were the Cherokees annihilated, but their leader and Houston's friend, Chief Bowles, was killed. It was too much for Houston. He had been away in the United States at the time, and on his return, he found his political enemy, President Mirabeau B. Lamar had ordered the removal of the Cherokees from Texas. Using the excuse the Cherokees were in alliance with the Mexicans, Lamar sent an army to see that the Indians left their lands. In a furious speech of outrage and frustration Houston denounced Lamar's administration and infuriated his own colleagues when he called Chief Bowles "a better man than his murderers."

One of the greatest friends the Republic of Texas had during those dark days of struggle against Mexico was the Cherokee Nation. Under the leadership of Chief Bowles, the Cherokees signed a treaty with Sam Houston agreeing not to take arms against Texas, and in return they would be given title to their land, which they had been unable to get under Mexican rule. Bowles also tried to get the hostile tribes of West Texas to make peace, but when that effort failed, the Cherokee Chief offered to fight against the Comanches to help the Republic. Another show of honor

and friendship on the part of Bowles came during the Runaway Scrape. It would have been an easy matter for the Cherokees to cause further death and destruction, but the honorable Chief Bowles never once broke his word to Sam Houston.

Highly intelligent, the Cherokees were one of the Five Civilized Tribes forced to move westward from Mississippi and Alabama when the white men wanted their tribal lands.

Bowles and his followers crossed the Sabine about 1820. Bowles, the son of a Scotch-Irish father and Cherokee mother, with his reddish hair, gray eyes, and freckles was in his late sixties. The tribe entered into negotiations with Mexico for land in hope they would be given title to the rich fertile hills of East Texas. Their petitions were never acted upon, and the Cherokees were destined to never find a home in Texas. When the revolution was over, an ungrateful Texas Republic refused to ratify Houston's treaty with its promise of land for the tribe.

No sooner had Texas won its independence than avaricious men began looking for ways to move the Cherokees from the boundaries of the Republic. Their chance came in 1839 when two white families were attacked by Indians. During the Killough Massacre, eighteen were slain. Among the Indians killed in pursuit after the massacre was a Mexican agent named Manual Flores. On his body were papers proving Mexico was working to incite the Cherokees against Texas. Mexico had not recognized Texas' independence, and as far as Mexico was concerned, a state of war still existed. Some sources believe that Mexican agents were the cause of the Killough Massacre; certainly it had not been any of Bowles' warriors.

Regardless, tempers were high, and outrage dictated that the Indians must leave Texas. President Lamar, who was certainly no friend of any Indian, much less the Cherokees, ordered the removal of Bowles and his tribe "peaceably if they would, forcibly if they must."

The corn was ready for harvest, and the Cherokees demanded payment. Texas refused. There was also a clause in the treaty that the Indians must accept an armed escort out of Texas. This was an anathema to the proud Cherokees. Chief Bowles advised his people that they would lose, but the die was cast.

The battle of the Neches began on a blazing hot July afternoon in 1839. General Kelsey Douglass commanded about five hundred troops under Rusk, Burleson, and Landrum. Rather than fighting behind cover, the Indians formed a battle line. By sundown, eighteen Indians were dead and only three Texans, an omen of events to follow.

The next day the battle resumed. Mounted on a paint horse, Bowles was a magnificent specimen of barbaric manhood. Wearing his sword and sash and the military hat and silk vest given to him by Sam Houston, the Indian Chief was prepared for his death. Very much exposed, Bowles kept urging his warriors to charge, and he was the last one to retreat. As he finally turned his horse, the grand old man was shot in the back. He fell from his horse, walked forward a little, and fell again. Then, he somehow rose to a sitting position.

A Texas soldier described Bowles' death. "Wishing to save his life, I ran towards him, and, as I approached him from one direction, my captain, Robert Smith, approached him from another with his pistol drawn.

As we got to him, I said, 'Captain, don't shoot him' but as I spoke he fired, shooting the chief in the head, which caused instant death. It ought to be said for Captain Smith that he had known of the many murders and thefts by the Indians, and possibly did, in the heat of battle, what, under other circumstances, he would not have done, for he was esteemed as a most worthy man and citizen."

Just killing the old chief was not enough. The body was horribly mutilated. One "ghoulish wretch" cut strips of skin from Bowles and planned to make them into bridle reins. Then they scalped him, because according to tribal custom, funeral honors were paid only to unscalped braves. The desecrated body remained many years on the spot where Bowles had died. The murderer claimed the sword and hat.

The pursuit continued as fields were destroyed, huts burned, and more Indians killed. Most of the survivors fled to Cherokee lands outside of Texas, and a small group under Chief Egg and John Bowles, son of the dead chief, attempted during the winter to reach Mexico. Burleson, on a campaign against the plains Indians, intercepted the Cherokee braves on December 25, 1839, near the mouth of the San Saba River. Egg, Bowles, and several more were killed, and the women and children captured. That was the end of one of Texas' honorable allies. No wonder Sam Houston called his friend "a better man than his murderers."

"Those Like Humans"

**Tonkawa Indian
Scouts
Fort Griffin, 1840**

NOTHING REMAINS BUT blood-stained battlefields, a collection of rude arms, and the name of a small hamlet and an insignificant creek to remind us of one of the most loyal allies Texas ever had—the Tonkawa Indian Scouts.

The Tonkawa (Tonk-a-way) were originally not one tribe, but many whose lands were around the Edwards Plateau, and called themselves, "those like humans." With their tattoos, bows, and long lances they were a formidable foe. In readying for war, the "Tonks" dipped their darts in mistletoe juice and painted their bodies in a crude fashion. Using a puddle of saliva in the hollow of his hand, a warrior mixed red, green, yellow, and ochre paint and applied it in reeking smears.

The Tonkawa were such skillful trackers and scouts they could ride through a sleeping camp without disturbing a soul. When they killed an enemy, the Tonks scalped their victim, ears and all, then cut a small piece of skin from each breast and ate it for "good medicine." Old Indian fighters asked for them for their superior skills, and army commanders valued them so highly they fed the Indians at their own personal expense. A few Tonks were more useful than two or three companies of regular soldiers. Their main enemy was traditionally the arrogant Comanches, so when the white man came, the Tonkawa were quick to ally with them against their longtime foe.

The August 1840 raid was one of massive proportions. Almost a thousand Comanche warriors were on the warpath against the white settlements. Chief Buffalo Hump's victims littered the Texas prairies as far south as Linnville on Lavaca Bay. Finally, loaded down with plunder and encumbered by a few thousand stolen horses, the bloodbath ended, and the triumphant savages turned back toward the Staked Plains.

What the cunning Comanches had not reckoned on was the swift organization of Texas forces under Burleson, Caldwell, and Felix Huston. As the thieving Comanches headed north along the Colorado River, the thirteen Tonkawa scouts under Chief Placido reported that the Indians would reach Plum Creek, not far from present-day Lockhart. The Texans waited. As the great hoard of Indians and horses approached, the Texans attacked. In their futile efforts to save their horses, the Comanches dispersed their strength and lost the battle. The Texans literally rode them down, killing eighty Indians during the violent retreat. The brave Tonks who had run on foot with Burleson for more than thirty miles were mounted again. Only one Texan lay dead. Huston wrote Chief Placido and his scouts a citation for bravery.

Again in May of 1858 the Tonks served Texas valiantly. Their leader, Ranger Rip Ford, was out after the Comanches across the Red River. Chief Placido and a hundred of his braves successfully destroyed a small encampment, but two of the Comanches escaped to alert the main body of Indians. Ford and his Tonks and regular soldiers followed in hot pursuit.

When the Comanches went to war, they did it with style. They were literally dressed "fit to kill." Faces were painted black and framed with magnificent feather headdresses or huge crowns of buffalo horns. Resplendent in their fierceness, 300 Comanches readied for battle with the approaching cavalry. Their leader, Iron Jacket, wore an ancient Spanish cuirass probably discarded by one of Coronado's weary conquistadors many centuries before.

With his armor reflecting the hot sun, Iron Jacket seemed as invulnerable as legends had boasted. It was quite a spectacle with the Comanche braves in their brilliant array flaunting their superiority over the rough and dull-looking Rangers. Then Iron Jacket rode out in all of his splendor and issued a challenge. It was the last thing he ever did. Spanish steel was no match for a Sharps' rifle. The Texans shot him and Iron Jacket died instantly.

The Rangers and Tonks charged. After an incredible seven hours of pursuit and battle, the Texans proved that the Comanche could be beaten on his own ground. Only when his horses were reeling with exhaustion did Ford cease his relentless chase and merciless fight.

No matter how valuable the Tonks were in the Indian Wars, they were still redskins, and the majority of Texans believed they should be on a reservation. When the Brazos Reservation was moved to Indian Territory in Oklahoma in 1859, Placido and his three hundred Tonkawa were exiled as well. In spite of an ungrateful Texas, Placido still refused to aid Union sympathizers at the outbreak of the Civil War. He stubbornly remained loyal to Texas, and the tribe declared for the Confederacy.

For this unswerving loyalty, in 1862 near Anadarko, Oklahoma, the Delaware, Shawnee and Caddo tribes massacred 137 of the remaining 300 Tonkawa. Chief Placido requested asylum in Texas for his pitiful few, and they returned to Fort Griffin, living on the mercy of the government.

There was one last engagement for the remnants of this faithful ally— Palo Duro. With their wide-brimmed low-crowned white sombreros to distinguish them from their enemy, the Tonkawa stalked their quarry, the great Comanche chief, Quanah Parker. Under the leadership of the masterful campaigner Ranald Mackenzie, the Tonks would have their last moment of glory in September of 1874.

The Staked Plains were vast and endless. Months could be spent searching for the elusive Comanche without ever finding their main camp. A captured Comanchero, Jose Tafoya, was "persuaded" to tell Mackenzie that the last stronghold of the Comanche was hidden in Palo Duro Canyon.

Sergeant John Charlton and two Tonks, Johnson and Job, reached this magnificent crevice that so dramatically carves its way through those flat level plains of the Panhandle. Deep at the foot of this beautiful canyon were the teepees, horses, and all the things a Comanche warrior valued in life. The Tonks had found the main Comanche force.

At sunrise on September 28, Ranald Mackenzie fought the last major battle of the Indian Wars in Texas. Crawling down the one trail into Palo Duro at the head of the troopers were the Tonkawa scouts. Leading their horses, Mackenzie and his men followed. The scouts worked well and quietly killed the sentries, but the camp was aroused. In Comanche fashion, the braves made a stand while the women and children escaped. In spite of Mackenzie's element of surprise, the Comanches made good their retreat with only four killed.

Pursuit was impossible, but it wasn't necessary. The Comanches were defeated anyway. They had left behind their teepees and supplies which Mackenzie burned. No doubt the Indians could have survived without those, but also trapped in Palo Duro were their horses. A mounted Comanche was a formidable foe indeed, but, without his horse, he was hardly better than a squaw. Mackenzie took the expedient step and slaughtered all the horses. It was the end of one of the greatest fighting forces in Texas. The Comanche would never be an awesome threat again.

It was also the end for the Tonkawa. Scouts were no longer needed, so in 1884 what few Tonks were left were assigned to the Oakland Agency in Ponca City, Oklahoma. Here they lived as poverty-stricken rural workers and were gradually absorbed into other tribes.

In the history of settling Texas there was never room for the Indian whether he was a friend or enemy. When the Texans' allies were no longer necessary, they were simply cast out. The Cherokees, the Seminoles, the Tonkawa—once they committed to the Texas cause they remained loyal. Their loyalty was rewarded with expulsion and extinction.

She Never Forgot

W HEN YOU HEAR THE story of Indian Emily, you can close your eyes and visualize the perfect Hollywood western scenario. This tearful tale has every ingredient a scriptwriter could wish—unrequited love, betrayal, self-sacrifice, and tragic death. Even the setting is as perfect today as it was during those turbulent years on the Texas frontier. Fort Davis was one of a line of forts established by the U.S. government to protect the steady stream of gold seekers and pioneers heading west.

Many stories are told about this important fort, for here the entire frontier history is encapsulated in one small point of command. Fort Davis was even unique in that it was part of the great Camel Experiment that Jefferson Davis instigated. Davis believed the "ships of the Sahara Desert" could easily become "ships of the Chihuahuan Desert." This major innovation was totally successful, but unfortunately the year was 1860–1861, and Jefferson Davis would have an influence on the nation's decisions from an entirely different perspective.

Fort Davis was abandoned during the Civil War and left to the Indians. When the war was over, the fort was reorganized and amazingly retained

Indian Emily
Fort Davis, 1867

the name of the rebel Confederate president. By 1867 Fort Davis was once again an important outpost against Indian depredations, particularly the Apaches.

The year was 1867 and a wagon train was headed for the Davis Mountains. They chose to camp not far from the fort with plans to arrive with their badly needed supplies the next day. It was a fateful mistake. At sunrise the Apaches attacked in force, and after a devastating fight, the Indians were repulsed. Among the dead and dying Indians was a wounded young Indian girl. She was taken in and nursed back to health by a kindly Mrs. Easton, the mother of a young lieutenant, Tom Easton, stationed at the fort.

The lonely Mrs. Easton was delighted with her new companion and gave her the Christian name of Emily. Emily returned her benefactor's affection, but she felt a different emotion for Mrs. Easton's handsome son.

It was a hopeless love. Ambitious lieutenants certainly did not marry Indian squaws. They married pretty white girls whose father could help them up the military ladder. When the Nelsons arrived at Fort Davis with their lovely daughter Mary, it was just a matter of a few months before she wore Tom Easton's ring.

Emily's heart gave her no choice but to run away, and word finally came back to the fort that the girl Mrs. Easton had loved as her own was back with her people. Unaware of Emily's secret love for her son, the kindly woman was heartbroken and puzzled by Emily's abrupt disappearance. Time passed, but Mrs. Easton never forgot her Indian daughter. Emily had never forgotten her white mother or her secret love, either.

One dark night an alert sentry heard a suspicious noise and saw a vague form in the gloom. "Halt or I'll shoot!" he commanded, but there was no reply. "Halt!" he called again and the figure moved faster. Then the soldier fired!

Even in the black of night the sentry's aim was true. They bore Emily to the fort, and the dying girl called for her benefactress. When Mrs. Easton reached her side Emily's last words were for her secret love, "My people come—I hear talk—Lieutenant Tom no get killed—goodbye."

Emily's warning indeed saved Tom Easton and the fort. The sentry was spared as well, and when he told the story of that sad night, he kept remembering how the "Injun girl kept coming—like she wanted me to shoot."

For years in the old fort cemetery stood a plain, rude cross with the forlorn statement, "Emily, the Indian Squaw." Finally, that disappeared, but in 1936 in honor of its centennial, Texas remembered Emily and placed a fine stone marker over her grave.

To relive the story of the Indian girl's tragic love, go out to old Fort Davis in the beautiful Davis Mountains. It has been so authentically restored you can hardly believe its years of glory are gone forever. You can even hear a dress review with its snap commands and military music filling the parade grounds, for they are broadcast at timed intervals. And if you take the cemetery path, over the hill under a large tree is a single stone with the words,

> Here lies Indian Emily, an Apache girl whose love for a young officer induced her to give warning of an Indian attack. Mistaken for an enemy, she was shot by a sentry, but saved the garrison from massacre.

The First Cattle Baron

Colonel Jack Myers
Lockhart, 1867

IT IS UNCANNY HOW often momentous decisions are reached in one brief encounter. But, two men of great vision and daring happened to meet in Junction City, Kansas, and the bargain they struck would have an incredible effect on Texas and its struggle to overcome the blows of the Civil War.

After the War Between the States, literally millions of unbranded Longhorn cattle roamed the Texas grasslands. This tough breed had adapted perfectly to the new world so far from their original pastures in Spain. These untamed ornery Longhorns were money on the hoof, but were without a market. (See *Traveling Texas Borders*, Lone Star Books, Houston.)

In 1866 a brash Yankee named Joseph C. McCoy headed west to make his fortune. McCoy envisioned a town of endless loading pens at the railhead to hold cattle destined for the hungry northern markets. Was this dream actually feasible? Would enough Texans endure the hardships of the trail to get their cattle to market? He felt confident he could convince the railroad to push its tracks farther west if he could deliver the cattle for shipment.

By a fortuitous twist of fate McCoy arrived in Junction City, Kansas, to begin this bold new venture just as Colonel Jack Myers also was re-

turning to town after a trail drive from Lockhart, Texas, to the Mormons in Utah. No other cattleman knew as much about the territory and cattle than Jack Myers. He had been with Fremont when the territory was mapped and had driven herds long before the famous trails were begun. McCoy and Myers made a formidable team.

The two men strolled to a lumber pile on a vacant lot. They sat on a stack of boards and for two hours McCoy listened intently to the opinions of the Texas drover. The Yankee questioned, "If I build these pens, will you bring me 25,000 head of cattle a year?"

The Colonel replied in all sincerity, "We will bring you a million head a year."

There are moments in one's existence when a decision or a purpose shapes all future actions and events. Such was the effect of these brief two hours, for McCoy felt he had been speaking with a sincere, honest man who knew what he was talking about.

McCoy went on to found the rip-roaring cowtown of Abilene, Kansas, and Myers went back to Lockhart to round 'em up and head 'em out. It was this veteran of the Confederate Army that would mark the Texas-Oklahoma part of the legendary Chisholm Trail when he drove the first herd up to Abilene in 1867. The partnership of Myers and McCoy began the mystique of the Texas cowboy and changed the destiny of the state forever.

Until 1875 Myers annually arrived in Abilene with 4,000 to 16,000 head of bawling Longhorns. They fought the elements to Fort Worth, survived the crossing of the mighty Red River, and made their way through the Indian Nations of Oklahoma to arrive with incredible stories of life on the trail.

Myers was good as his word. Millions, not thousands, of head of cattle made their torturous way to the railhead. They made wealthy men of hungry cattlemen, and the great ranches of Texas were created. Perhaps, best of all, this brief era gave Texas a special place in the history of the west. Men who made the drives spun tales that will live on in story and song forever.

This Texan so instrumental in shaping the destiny of the Lone Star State was once described as "a man that has few enemies, but his name is spoken with respect, akin to love and admiration. He is a man true to his pledge and one who would not take advantage or oppress a fellowman."

As life is filled with ironies, this true son of Texas was murdered by chloroform poisoning in Omaha, Nebraska. He had just delivered a large herd, and thieves killed him for his money. For nine years he had made the great drives, and his body now rests in Lockhart, the beginning of the Chisholm Trail he had pioneered.

The Most Effective Fighting Force on the Texas Frontier

I N A SCRUFFY GRAVEYARD just south of Brackettville lie the remains of one of the most effective fighting forces on the Texas frontier, the Seminole-Negro scouts. From the 1870s until the early 1900s this superior troop of trackers were always able to trail the wily Comanches and Apaches. The scouts were hardly distinguishable racially from other blacks, but they were all Indian in their trailing, hunting, and fighting abilities. These descendents of runaway slaves and the Florida Seminole Indians were an effective force far out of proportion to their number, for there were never more than fifty men under command at any one time.

During and after the Civil War the Plains tribes had become so adept at stealing it was impossible to track them down. Finally the U.S. Cavalry coerced the remnant of the Seminole-Negroes to return from Mexico where they had fled in preference to being put on a reservation. Under terms of "de treaty," they would receive pay and a grant of land for their service. The scouts furnished their own horses and dressed in a modified Indian style, but they were issued Spencer carbines.

Lieutenant John Lapham Bullis was given the command of this unique troop. Small in stature, Bullis was a thin, spare wiry man with a large black mustache, and his face was burned as red as an Indian's. Bullis conducted affairs with his scouts more like a war chief with his braves rather than in a conventional officer-soldier relationship. The leader and his troops had a mutual admiration and confidence, which was inestimably important for the success of the scouts.

Called the "Whirlwind" and the "Thunderbolt," the lieutenant endured the same hardships and ate the same rations as his men. Both officer and scouts had the ability to stay on the trail for months at a time and subsist indefinitely on half-rations, and live off the land. According to re-

The Seminole-Negro Scouts Brackettville, 1875

ports, Bullis' idea of a luxurious march was to put a single can of corn in his haversack, and if he did have rations, he made it a rule to live on one can of food a day. It was a severe ordeal for soldiers of other companies to keep up with the rapidly moving Seminoles, so usually they operated independently of each other.

The feats of Bullis and his men were incredible. One that was worthy of a Remington painting occurred on April 25, 1875. Lieutenant Bullis with Sergeant John Ward, Trumpeter Isaac Payne, and Trooper Pompey Factor were trailing about seventy-five stolen horses and came upon the Indians as they were attempting to cross the Pecos River. Tethering their mounts, the scouts crept up to within a few yards and opened fire, killing three warriors. Eventually, however, the Comanches discovered the small number of their attackers and worked around until they almost cut the scouts off from their horses. Bullis and his men had to run for their lives.

Reaching their horses, the scouts mounted and were getting away when Sergeant Ward looked back and saw that Bullis' wild and badly trained horse had broken loose leaving him on foot to face the triumphant Indians. "We can't leave the lieutenant, boys!" Ward cried. Wheeling his horse, the sergeant dashed back with his comrades following. A bullet cut Ward's carbine sling as he reached Bullis and helped him mount behind. Now, firing right and left, the three scouts and the rescued officer rode again through the band of thirty Indians and, as Bullis wrote, "saved my hair." This stirring feat of bravery won the scouts the Congressional Medal of Honor.

In October of 1875 Lieutenant Bullis and Sergeant Miller, who looked white, acted like an Indian, but was actually a mulatto, crept into an Indian camp and stole thirty horses and mules. The next year Miller boldly entered an Indian camp in Mexico in disguise and remained five days.

On another raid, Bullis and twenty scouts with Negro cavalrymen trailed a band of Lipans 110 miles in twenty-four hours. At daybreak the scouts charged into the sleeping camp. In the wild confused melee the fighting was chiefly hand to hand with carbines used as clubs against the long Lipan lances. In fifteen minutes four Indians were dead and the scouts had their horses back.

In dozens of encounters with Indians over eight years not a single Seminole scout was killed or even seriously injured. They were not so lucky in their encounters with the Texas citizenry. Several scouts were killed in a conflict over some land near Fort Clark, and another was bushwacked by a sheriff who suspected him of murder. Some of the scouts got disgusted and washed the dust of Texas from their horses' hooves and crossed the Rio Grande back to Mexico. But, the majority of the scouts were loyal, if not so much to the United States then at least to Bullis.

By 1877 Bullis and his band were constantly on the trail. The enemy was growing wary and was hard to capture. While on one foray, Bullis and his scouts were caught on a narrow ledge in a deep canyon of the Big Bend by Mescaleros. "Even though greatly outnumbered, by their wiles and courage succeeded in extricating themselves" read the report. They then sent for reinforcements, and picked up the trail again, although twenty-three days had passed. They left their horses and walked over a mountain to surprise the enemy camp. The scouts then killed the thieving chief and retrieved thirty horses and mules.

The feats of Bullis and his men border on the unbelievable. Not even Hollywood could capture the spirit, courage, and tenacity of this rare fighting force. On the trail of some Mescalero raiders they were nearly perishing with thirst when Sergeant David Bowlegs displayed an uncanny desert craft by discovering a "sleeping spring" which the hostiles had stopped up and hidden. By the greatest care and skill Bowlegs made the spring flow freely again and saved their lives. Although Bullis and his pursuers tracked the Mescaleros to Fort Stanton, New Mexico, the Indian agent there refused to give them up, and the scouts returned empty handed. In 80 days they had covered an incredible 1,266 miles.

A few descendents of these amazing fighters are still living around Del Rio and the Whitehead Museum has a small exhibit of their exploits, but Texas has yet to fully honor the daring deeds of these Seminole-Negro scouts.

Head 'Em Up, Move 'Em Out

THERE WAS A BRIEF era in Texas history that has captured the imagination as no period before it or since. From 1865 until 1885 millions of head of ornery Longhorn cattle made their way up the fabled Texas trails to the hungry northern markets and created the truly American folk hero—the cowboy.

Old Blue
Palo Duro Canyon,
1880

In spite of all the glamor of cheap novels, Hollywood and television, the cowboy led a pretty miserable existence. This "only common laborer to become a symbol of heroism" endured the rigors of the trail—maurading Indians, rustlers, swollen rivers, heat, the interminable dust, a basic diet of biscuits and beans, sudden howling storms, and little or no sleep—for about a dollar a day.

Colonel Charles Goodnight of the legendary J A Ranch expressed trail driving being "the most pleasant work connected with the cattle business in the early days; if a man was trained to it, and liked to work, it was glorious work." J. W. Martin, an old trail hand saw life somewhat differently. He believed that the pleasure derived depended a great deal upon the kind of cattle you were driving as well as weather conditions.

"Two-year-old heifers are the meanest cattle in the world to drive," said Martin, "while most any kind of cattle are liable to stampede the first three or four days they are on the road, two-year-old heifers never get 'road broke.' I remember on one trip of twenty days, with it raining

most of the time, this bunch of two-year-old heifers ran every night, and as a result the boys were not in bed over four hours at a time." Obviously Colonel Goodnight had been spared many drives with two-year-old heifers.

One thing that was necessary for a successful trail drive with the least trouble was to have a good leader for the cattle to follow. The J A Ranch had such a leader, an old blue Texas steer that made himself as famous as the ranch. One of the hands, a Mr. Kent, gave the following tribute to Old Blue.

> In the early days, cattle were very wild and when they were started on the trail, after the first two or three days, there would be a few steers that would take the lead and keep it all the rest of the way. There was one old blue steer that always did this, so taking advantage of this fact, we would rope Old Blue and one of us boys would lead him in front and the rest of the herd would follow. I led him all the way from the J A Ranch to Dodge City, Kansas once, and some of the other boys did the same thing later. When we got ready to start back to the ranch, we would turn Old Blue loose and he would come back to the ranch with the cow horses. The fellow who led Old Blue had to swim all the rivers first, and this was a dangerous business when the rivers were swollen. Old Blue came in handy, too, in penning cattle. He was used for many purposes and finally died of old age. His horns are kept in the office of the J A headquarters over the door leading to the vault.

The J A Ranch was the result of a meeting between Charles Goodnight and John G. Adair, an Englishman who wanted to go into the cattle business. Adair agreed to furnish the money for two thirds of the property and profits with one third for Goodnight. With 12,000 acres purchased from Jot Gunter in Palo Duro Canyon, the J A became one of the most successful ranches in Texas.

Not only did Old Blue do his part to make the J A part of Texas history, the ranch paved the way for settlement of the inhospitable Panhandle High Plains. This whole saga is vividly brought to life each summer at Palo Duro Canyon with the professional outdoor pageant *Texas*. Old Blue isn't there, but others of his kind share the stage with the many colorful figures from Texas' wild and wooly Panhandle history.

V
Bullets and Arrows: The Indian Wars

The Red Baron

Baron Emil
Von Kriewitz
Llano, 1847

THE STORY OF THE German colonization of Texas is the story of John O. Meuseback, Prince Carl of Solms-Braunfels, and the *Adelsverein*. But, there is another elusive character who makes a brief appearance time and again in the history of these early German pioneers. Facts about Baron Emil Von Kriewitz's past are sketchy, and even details of his long life in Texas are brief, but he did render a great service to his fellow Germans on the frontier.

When the *Adelsverein* was organized by German nobility in 1842 for the purpose of purchasing Texas land and promoting immigration, they acquired a large track known as the Fisher-Miller Grant which lay between the Llano and San Saba Rivers. Upon arrival in Texas the colonists found their land was right in the heart of Comanche territory. The grant was worthless for it would be suicide to settle among one of the most hostile tribes in the new Republic.

Baron Ottfried Hans Freiherr Von Meusebach (Moyse-bach), the leader of the German immigrants, had succeeded Prince Carl of Solms-Braunfels as commissioner general of Texas Germans. This brilliant employee of the *Adelsverein* dropped his title of nobility to become plain John O. Meusebach and dedicated his life to the welfare of his German Texans.

One of Meusebach's most succesful coups was a peace treaty negotiated with the Comanches in 1847. According to the terms of the treaty the Germans could settle in Comanche territory, the Comanches would protect them from other tribes and permit land surveys and boundaries to be established. In return the Germans would maintain the peace and give them $1,000 worth of presents. That $1,000 was one of the best investments the Germans ever made, for both sides honored their terms, and there was never a Comanche attack made on their settlements.

There was one other stipulation to the treaty by the Comanches. The Germans must send an agent to live among them as a guaranty of good faith. At the next full moon the Comanche chiefs were to come to Fredericksburg for their presents and to the meet the man who was to serve as the mediator between them.

Chief Santa Anna and his braves arrived in Fredericksburg at the appointed time and received his promised gifts. A lively exchange took place between both parties, and the Indians even took part in laying the cornerstone for the church. Meusebach's strategy had worked.

Among the Germans was another baron who had come to try his luck in the new land. Emil Von Kriewitz had been with Meusebach when the treaty was negotiated and had given the matter of the agent considerable thought. In his own words the ex-nobleman wrote, "I decided to risk my scalp because the safety of the proposed colonies along the Llano River and of Fredericksburg depends on the friendliest possible relationship with the Indians."

Kriewitz left a grateful Fredericksburg for a life totally unimaginable to the civilized colonists. When this brave German arrived at the main camp of Santa Anna, Kriewitz informed the chief as best he could through gestures and broken Spanish that he had come to live with them as an Indian and he would serve both sides fairly. Kriewitz had his chance to prove himself almost immediately.

At Waco, a trader called One-Eye Barnett feared his business would shift to Fredericksburg because of the treaty. Barnett told the Comanches the Germans would take their land and horses, but Kriewitz convinced the Comanches of the Germans' honor and good faith, and trouble was avoided.

After a few months, the Indians wanted more presents and became demanding. Santa Anna declared it was time to pay "El Sol Colorado" (Meusebach was called "The Red Sun" for his flaming red beard) a visit. Nothing Kriewitz could do would stop them. Santa Anna and his followers left San Saba and rode to New Braunfels, the first and last time Indians were ever in this German town. Kriewitz was with them, dressed like a savage, but no one recognized their fellow German, so completely had he adopted the Comanche way of life. When one of the settlers realized the ex-baron was not an Indian, Kriewitz touched him under the table with his foot and secretly handed him a piece of paper with "Kriewitz" written on it. The Germans understood.

For a quarter of a century Kriewitz remained with the Comanches. He even achieved the honorary status of chief, and Santa Anna became his close friend. After the Comanches had been defeated and forced to settle on Reservations, the baron washed the war paint from his body and returned to his people with as much indifference as if he had been away on a hunt. He married a German lady and settled in Castell as its postmaster.

Among the many treaties made and broken by the white men with their red adversaries, that made by the Germans and the Comanches is truly unique. The Comanches raided incessantly over Texas, even as far south as Port Lavaca, but they never harmed their German brothers. To Emil Kriewitz goes a great deal of the credit for this unusual peace. German families were always reassured with, "Don't be afraid, the baron will not let the Indians harm his people." They were right. Kriewitz did his duty well.

The Ordeal of Ed Westfall

**Ed Westfall
Uvalde, 1850**

E D WESTFALL WAS A dead man. He had dared to live on Comanche land. Now he would pay for his effrontery. Westfall's isolated rude cabin on the Leona River was surrounded by savages intent on killing him. His only companion, a French trapper named Louis, had been hit in the chest and lay dead by the doorway. The nearest help at Fort Inge was thirty desolate miles away. There was no way out. No escape. No hope. Death was merely a matter of time.

All day the Comanches had maintained their siege on the lone white man. To cross the clearing meant instant death because of Westfall's remarkable aim. So they waited. Suddenly, a chance shot hit Westfall in the neck. Blind and choking on his blood, in one last desperate bluff the wounded Westfall wedged his rifle through the logs as if he were ready to pick off the next warrior that dared the clearing. Almost senseless, the

Ed Westfall was a dead man, but he refused to die. With utmost courage and an extraordinary will, he survived the Comanche attack.

rancher fell on the bed. Yet, in his pain and anguish he knew if he rolled on his back he would strangle on his blood.

When he regained consciousness, whether a day or a week had passed Westfall had no way of knowing. All he knew was that for some mysterious reason the Indians were gone, and he had a chance. If he could walk or crawl those agonizing thirty miles to the fort, his life might be saved. A lesser man may have realized the hopelessness of the situation, but not Ed Westfall. He was a true frontiersman, and he would fight regardless of the odds against him. Somehow Westfall managed to drag Louis's body from the door, and begin his ghastly journey.

One of Westfall's best friends was the legendary scout Bigfoot Wallace. Bigfoot was credited with superhuman powers, and perhaps his biographers were right, for as he rode to the Leona River, Bigfoot was gripped with a dreadful premonition that something was wrong, terribly wrong. Bigfoot had spent many years fighting Indians, and when he reached Westfall's cabin he realized immediately what had happened. When the Ranger saw the bloody bed, he believed someone had died. No time now to bury the Frenchman. He had to find his friend, dead or alive.

The trail was easy to follow, too easy. Wallace could tell from the marks in the dirt how his friend was suffering. Would he reach Ed in time? Bigfoot could even see where the dazed and blinded man had fallen, where he had been overcome by agony, almost unable to move. Yet, somehow Westfall had managed to keep moving. The tracker feared desperately what he would find ahead on the trail as he followed his injured friend. Moving carefully, Bigfoot did not want to pass Westfall by if the injured man had crawled off in the brush to die.

Through an incredible will to live, Westfall made it those thirty endless miles to the fort all alone. When Bigfoot found his friend, Westfall was lying in the fort hospital unconscious, but alive. How had he done it? The bullet had not only grazed Ed's jugular vein, but it had creased his lung. Ed should have been a dead man seven days ago when he was hit.

Ed Westfall arrived in Texas in 1845 as a young man of twenty-five and volunteered for service in the Mexican War. Here he met the famous William A. A. "Bigfoot" Wallace, and they became lifelong friends. When Wallace carried the mail to El Paso, Westfall rode as his guard. When Wallace raised a company of Texas Rangers for defense, his friend became his lieutenant.

A formal education was indeed a rarity among men like Westfall and Wallace, but Ed loved to read and he kept journals. This intense love of knowledge of the frontiersman was reflected in his will. Ed requested that at his wife's death, his money would then go to build a library in San Antonio. Today, it is doubtful if more than a handful of patrons of the Westfall Branch of the San Antonio Public Library know who their benefactor was.

Ed Westfall was a courageous man and one of the bravest of the brave, but this modest man did not want to be remembered for his daring exploits on the frontier, and it is very probable he did not care if he were remembered at all. But, if the world must know about Ed Westfall, he would want them to remember him for his gift of knowledge to those who loved books as he did.

The Indian's Agent

Major Robert S.
Neighbors
Fort Belknap, 1859

IT WAS EXCEEDINGLY HOT on that July day of 1859 as the caravan of homeless Lipan Apache and Tonkawa tribes turned their faces toward the Nations of Oklahoma and their new reservation. Suddenly, a shower of rain fell, and it seemed the clouds wept the tears the Indians were too stoical to shed. During the terrible two weeks on the trail most of the livestock and some of the elderly Indians had died. Escorted by soldiers and Rangers, the Indians were forced to leave behind their homes and their land for the white man. They were led by Robert S. Neighbors, a man who had more influence over Texas Indians than any other man in the history of the Lone Star State.

A Virginian by birth, Neighbors came to Texas in 1836. Captured by General Adrian Woll at San Antonio in 1842, he was held in the infamous Perote Castle for two years. Upon Neighbors' release, he was appointed by President Anson Jones in 1845 as Indian agent for the Lipan Apache and Tonkawa tribes.

For the rest of his life Neighbors worked to prevent the extermination of the Indians. The agent saw them as humans defending a doomed way of life. Nothing would stop the white man from taking the land they saw as theirs, and nothing would stop the red man from defending to the death the land he thought was his. There was no way Neighbors would escape the title "Indian lover."

This big, strong, immensely courageous man was patient with Indians and angrily impatient with white prejudices. Naturally he could not win or hold confidence of the Indians without losing that of the whites. Two years after his appointment as agent, Neighbors wrote that the whites gave him more trouble than the Indians. The whites would cross the Indians' boundaries and troops would not bother to discriminate between friendly and hostile Indians. Nor was there a law to prevent civilians from dealing with the Indians.

Major Neighbors found the Tonkawa on the San Marcos River living a miserable existence. They were oppressed by the whites on one side and by the arrogant Comanches on the other. This once powerful tribe had been reduced to subsisting on fish, roots, snakes, and other reptiles. After he had been with the Tonkawa long enough to acquire their confidence he found their aversion to farming was religious in nature. In their most sacred rite celebrating the origin of the tribe, the Tonkawas believed they were descendents of the wolf. Henceforth a warrior must make his livelihood as the wolves did, by killing and stealing and wandering place to place. Even as much as the Tonkawa admired and trusted Neighbors, they never wholeheartedly accepted farming as a way of life.

Neighbors was honest, God-fearing, and ethical, and gained even the trust of the fierce Comanches. One day Comanche braves led by Old

The Texas Rangers hated
Robert Neighbors, and
the white men called him
an Indian lover, but his
untiring efforts saved the
red man from extinction.

Owl rode into the Tonkawa camp to harass their enemies. The agent saw a rare opportunity to establish friendly relations with the Comanches. He explained his functions as Indian agent and expressed the desire of his government for peace. Old Owl replied that the whites were all great rascals, but he liked the Major and especially admired his coat. The agent understood, and took off his coat and presented it to the chief. Then the other braves began admiring his pants and other portions of his clothing. Soon the Major was stripped of all but his shirt. He began to laugh heartily at the comical appearance of the Comanche warriors as they strutted about with odd pieces of his clothing on their bodies. The Comanches were so pleased with Neighbors's generosity they proposed adopting him into their tribe and making a good horse thief out of him.

When Texas joined the Union, Neighbors was appointed as the Federal agent for the Indians. The settlers wanted the Indians exterminated, but through superhuman efforts the dedicated agent achieved the almost impossible feat of moving the Indians to the Brazos Reservation.

War bands continued to roam the country attacking settlers, and the reservation Indians were blamed. Neighbors was hated by the Texas Rangers. They could not understand a white man who stood up for Indian rights. The only solution as Neighbors saw it was to remove the Indians north of the Red River to protect them from the whites.

The agent went to Washington to plead his case, and the matter was brought to a head when six white men murdered seven Indians. The Rangers would not arrest the offenders claiming they were civilians and not Ranger business. It was obvious the Indians must be removed to the Red River immediately and Neighbors was in charge of this arduous trek to a distant home. Had it not been for the work of agent Neighbors and the trust the Indians placed in him, there might have been even more deaths along the way.

On August 14, 1859, as Neighbors was returning from his sad journey, he met a senseless death at the hands of murderer Edward Cornett. Cornett said he resented some comments Neighbors had made about the recent killing of an Indian by white men. When Cornett was brought to trial the proceedings were interrupted by the alarm that Cornett's wife had been captured by Indians. The court rushed out in pursuit only to find it was a ruse to stop the trial. However, Cornett was never brought to trial again. The trick had worked.

A few months later Cornett's body was found in the Belknap hills. One account says that Ben R. Milam and John Crochan tracked Cornett and when he "made fight" Neighbors' murderer was brought to justice.

Ransom and Rescue

**Britt Johnson
Graham, 1864**

DURING THOSE BITTER YEARS of the Confederacy, the Texas frontier was at the complete mercy of the Indians. Forts had been abandoned, and Texans now wore the gray uniform, for there was a much greater cause at stake far to the east. Many a defenseless settlement suffered from marauding savages, and one of the most brutal attacks was the Elm Creek raid in October 1864.

Led by Chief Little Buffalo, the Comanches surrounded the undefended Fitzpatrick cabin. Trapped inside were several women and children, including the wife and three children of a black man named Britt Johnson. Although legally a slave, Britt was respected by everyone and allowed to live as a freedman.

As the savages circled the log cabin, one of the women, Susan Durgan rashly grabbed a gun and rushed outside. The poor girl was cut down immediately and the Indians stripped and mutilated her body. The other women and children were then taken hostage, but when two of the savages quarreled over which one had captured Britt's boy, they brutally killed the child to settle the argument. The rest of the captives were thrown on horses and carried away.

When Britt arrived at the ghastly scene and found his son dead and his family missing, the black man vowed he would find his wife and other two children. The next spring this devoted husband rode out into Indian territory all alone on his almost impossible quest.

Britt made three trips during his search and finally came across a lone Indian who could "talk Mexican." He learned the Comanches had a white woman, but the Kiowas had some black captives. More Indians rode up, and the black man joined this war band for several weeks. The Indians admired their new friend so much they agreed to help Britt ransom his family.

Finally, in a Comanche camp on the Canadian River, Britt found Mrs. Elizabeth Fitzpatrick. Sadly the grief-stricken woman told the story of how her son had been killed because he could not keep up. She begged Johnson to get her and the other captives back, and she would pay any price. Britt readily agreed and was successful in ransoming them from his Comanche friends.

Milky Way, the Comanche Chief, was so impressed with Britt he told the huge black man how to bargain with the tricky Kiowas. Milky Way even sent two braves with him to the Kiowa camp.

Once again Britt was lucky. The black captives were his family, and following Milky Way's advice, Britt ransomed them for about $2.50. The cunning Kiowas had been outsmarted in the bargaining.

One of Britt's great delights was to tell of his adventures among the Comanches and Kiowas. But, the vengeful Kiowas never forgave or forgot how they had been outbargained. One day in 1871 Britt and two black companions were freighting a wagon train when a large force of painted warriors attacked. His two companions fell early, but Britt was determined not to give up his life easily. He deliberately cut the throat of his horse and made a breastwork of its carcass. When the three blacks' mutilated bodies were found, Britt had left 173 empty shells around him. He had fought valiantly to the end.

The Frontier Was Not for the Weak or Cowardly

Ann Whitney and Amanda Howard Hamilton, 1867

THE SETTLING OF THE frontier is filled with horror stories of Indian depredations and untold numbers of their victims fill unmarked graves. It took raw courage to be a pioneer and true dedication to be a pioneer schoolteacher. For, in addition to all of the unknown hazards of beginning a new life in hostile territory, teachers faced the eternal problems of recalcitrant and listless students. Theirs was a hard life indeed.

One hot blistering July afternoon in 1867 Miss Ann Whitney was endeavoring to keep the attention of her sleepy students. The small log schoolhouse in Hamilton County was built on a rise overlooking the beautiful Warlene Valley. No obstacle marred the view from the schoolhouse door. As was the custom in those early days, the logs were unhewn and the spaces between were not filled. A small unshuttered window was cut in the north side of the rude one-room school. The closest homes were the Howards' a half mile west, and the Baggetts' a half mile to the east.

As Miss Whitney sat at her desk she noticed the little Powers girl gazing intensely out of the doorway. When the slightly irate teacher asked what she was staring at, the child answered, "There's a party of men coming, and they're Indians!"

Without taking the trouble to see for herself, Ann Whitney said, "Take your seat, child. It's Mr. Barbee coming for Olivia."

But the excited girl screamed, "They are Indians," and she grabbed her little brother and the two escaped through the small window.

The terrified teacher rushed to the door to see eleven Indians stealing her fine saddle horse, Mary. Ann had often made the remark, "If the Indians ever take Mary, I want them to take me, too." Little did she realize the horrible irony of those joking words. Frantically, she herded the children out of the window, and all made their escape except Mary Jane Manning, Olivia Barbee, and two of the Kuykendall boys. Those who got out scurried under the schoolhouse and were forced to witness the tragedy that followed. Miss Whitney weighed about 230 pounds, so her escape through the small window was impossible.

The Indians surrounded the rude cabin, and one who seemed to be the leader shouted in fair English, "Damn you, we have got you now!" Ann Whitney read her doom in those hideously painted faces of the bloodthirsty savages. Yet, somehow this heroic woman kept her presence of mind and begged the Indians to kill her if blood was what they wanted, but to spare the children.

The leader then held up three fingers and the Indians began shooting at the huge defenseless woman through the spaces between the logs with arrows and seldom missed their target. Mary Jane Manning clung hysterically to the skirts of her beloved teacher as blood gushed from Ann's numerous wounds and poured through the cracks in the floor to the trapped children underneath. Even as she was dying with an arrow in her back, Ann kept pleading with the savages to spare the children. Somehow she had managed to get the little Manning girl out of the window to safety before the Indians burst down the door. At least the brave teacher died before any more torture could be inflicted.

Quivering with fear, the two boys were asked if they wanted to go with their captors. One in fright said yes; the other refused. Strangely, with a "damn you, sit there," they left the one who said "no" alone, but took the one who said yes. Olivia also was dragged from the schoolhouse and put on a horse, but she managed to escape when the Indian turned away. The poor little girl was found the next day in shock, but she did recover. The kidnapped boy was later purchased from his abductors and returned home. None of the children hidden under the floor were hurt. The only victim of this hideous scene was the schoolteacher.

Meanwhile in the same valley another young woman was performing a courageous deed and saving the lives of the settlers. Amanda Howard and her sister-in-law, Sarah, rode into the valley as the Indians were murdering Ann Whitney. Amanda's horse was not completely tamed, and she was in the process of gentling the spirited animal. Sarah was just along keeping her company.

Just as the two girls spied the Indians, two braves galloped toward them. Amanda's horse refused to turn, and when she finally got the untrained steed to yield, she could see the terrible eyes of the Indians almost upon her. She dashed from her pursuers and headed straight for the Baggett's fences. Furiously lashing her mount, the horse easily cleared the barrier. Sarah did not fare so well. One of the Indians caught her horse, and she was thrown headlong over the fence but escaped to the Baggett's house.

But, more horror was to come in this afternoon of death. A Mr. Strangeline, his wife, a young daughter, and a baby entered the west end of the valley. Yelling like banshees, the Indians attacked the helpless family and killed the father instantly. The rest were all hit by arrows, but miraculously they were not killed.

The seventeen-year-old Amanda saw the attack on the Strangelines and the brave girl knew the settlers must be warned. To do this she must ride obliquely in the direction of the Indians. Galloping furiously, once again she cleared the fence. The Indians instantly saw through her daring plan and ceased their attack on the Strangelines, thereby saving the lives of the mother and children. Those Indians still at the schoolhouse also saw what Amanda planned to do, and all rushed pell mell to stop her mad dash for help. Here is an early account of Amanda Howard's courage:

> Picture, if you can, reader, a woman, surounded by hideously fiendish looking foes, thirsting and panting for her blood, she begging to be killed if that would save innocent childhood! And, again, a woman, riding into the very jaws of death, depending alone upon her skill in managing an unbroken horse, not bridlewise, and

the speed she may be able to get from him, to carry the news of the presence of savage foes to distant settlements! Thank heaven Miss Howard escaped by a few rods and the cowardly foe hurriedly turned westward carring the Kuykendall boy with them.

Amanda Howard's feat of courage saved many lives. The Indians fled, and even though the settlers tried to track them down to rescue the boy, the savages were not to be found.

The frontier was not for the weak and cowardly, but so often many of these early pioneers acted above the call of simple courage, and as with Ann Whitney and Amanda Howard, their heroism should never be forgotten.

"Squaw Much Brave"

Mrs. Crawford
Bastrop, 1873

N O ONE KNOWS HER first name. She's known only as Mrs. Crawford, a courageous pioneer woman determined to save her children. In the depths of despair a bedraggled woman stood captive surrounded by wild savages. Somehow she and her two small children had been spared when the settlement was attacked by Indians. Six people were killed, and among them was her husband. She had been beaten, kicked, and starved and her two-month-old baby was crying furiously to be fed.

Two Indians tired of the baby's crying and jerked him from his mother's arms and threw the helpless infant into a deep pool. The frantic mother immediately jumped in and saved her baby from drowning. No sooner had she climbed out than the cruel Indians seized the baby and threw it back. As fast as the mother could get her baby out of the water, her tormentors threw it back.

When Mrs. Crawford was totally exhausted, the Indians luckily tired of their game. Just as she thought her baby was safe, one of the warriors grabbed it, pulled its head back, and told another brave to cut the infant's tiny throat. It was too much for the distraught mother. Forgetting all danger, Mrs. Crawford picked up a heavy piece of wood, and with an amazing inner strength, the brave woman knocked the bloodthirsty savage to the ground.

Clutching her baby and trembling with fear, the mother waited for the death blow that was sure to come. Suddenly, the other Indians started laughing at the warrior she had struck. She couldn't believe her ears. They thought her act of sheer desperation was funny. The leader came to the terrified woman and said, "Squaw much brave." They never touched her or her child again.

For two horrible years Mrs. Crawford and her children were held captive, but her story had a happy ending. They were finally ransomed at Coffee's trading post on the Red River for 400 yards of calico and a number of blankets. Among the escort that took her back to friends was a Mr. Spaulding, who was so impressed by the widow's courage, he fell in love with her. After two years of living a nightmare, this indomitable woman faced the frontier again, this time as Mrs. Spaulding.

Medal of Honor (Two)

I T WAS A COLD, frosty morning that November 8 day in 1874. Lieutenant Baldwin of the 5th U.S. Infantry was performing hazardous duty as he convoyed twenty-three six-mule-team wagons through a section of country overrun by hostiles. Every eye was wary, for somewhere the great Comanche war chief Grey Beard was camped with all of his braves. In a recent raid the Comanches had taken two young girls hostage, and the soldiers wanted them back. The train had been a great impediment, but Baldwin had moved as rapidly as possible with his infantry in the wagons and followed no trails.

On that bitter November day the scouts were sent out at daybreak. Just as the train was ready to get moving, Scout Schmakle raced into camp at

Frank Dwight Baldwin McClellan's Creek, Gray County, 1874

breakneck speed. "Grey Beard! Grey Beard! Hundreds of Indians! Just over the rise!" yelled the excited scout.

Baldwin quickly dispatched the scout to General Miles at the fort with the message: "We have the Comanche camp. The convoy will attack at once, although we are greatly outnumbered. We request you come at once."

It was rashness to attack without a mounted cavalry, but the Lieutenant knew his men and knew they would fight bravely. He also knew he had the element of surprise in his favor.

Baldwin quickly formed his fighting force in a single line with the wagon train and howitzer in the center. The lumbering wagon train was actually in the "front line" of attack. The hostiles' camp was less than a mile away, yet amazingly the Indians were totally unaware of the troops.

As Baldwin's wagons reached the crest of the divide, trumpeters sounded the charge. As the clear shrill notes of that thrilling call echoed through the valley, it was the Indians' first warning of danger. Every trooper and every wagon in this brilliant strategic maneuver rushed down the slope and into and through the Indian camp like a raging whirlwind. The charge was spectacular and most effective! Over the hill they rolled, the mules straining with all their might as their drivers cracked the whips over the beasts' heads. What a glorious sight! Twenty-three charging wagons! It was probably the first time where every man, hoof and wheel was used in the first onslaught on an enemy's camp.

There was a massive stampede as the Indians retreated. Baldwin's men pressed their advantage and did not stop at the Indians' camp, but raced on to where the warriors made a stand. Taking only the time necessary to reform the command, Baldwin had the howitzer brought to bear as his few mounted troops charged. It was too much for the Comanches. They retreated rapidly toward the Staked Plains to the west with Baldwin in pursuit. However, after twelve miles the soldiers were forced to halt due to the utter exhaustion of their animals.

When General Miles arrived on the scene with the cavalry he found 300 Indians dead, many captured poinies, and the two little girls saved. Baldwin's magnificent charge had resulted in an overwhelming victory.

Baldwin had already distinguished himself on the field of battle. During the Civil War he received the Medal of Honor for leading his company in a gallant charge against the Confederate foe. He was awarded his second Medal of Honor for this magnificent charge on the plains of Texas.

Baldwin remained in the army all of his life and continued to serve his country fully and well. When Major General Frank Dwight Baldwin was buried with honors in Arlington National Cemetery, Brigadier General W. C. Brown eulogized: "In the development of the Great West few names stand higher than that of Frank Dwight Baldwin, the only name which has ever appeared in the Army Register followed by M.H. (two)."

Woodman, Spare That Tree

Martin Fleming
Comanche, 1918

THE OLD MAN STOOD beside the massive old tree, loaded shotgun in hand, waving a clenched fist at the approaching workmen. The crowd gathered round waiting expectantly to see what Uncle Mart would do. Everyone knew the old pioneer, and they never thought of him as a violent man, but here he was livid with rage, and anything could happen. Comanche was normally a very quiet little town, so all of the excitement brought the entire populace out to see what was going on. Up until today workmen had been cutting down the trees to pave the square, and there certainly wasn't much to watch there. Now, one of the town's oldest citizens was causing one hellacious uproar.

"You won't cut down this tree!" the old man thundered. "To this tree I own my life, and no axe will ever touch it. If necessary, I'll use my number ten's!" That stopped them. The crowd waited expectantly. What was so important about this particular oak tree? With the breeze gently ruffling his white hair, Uncle Mart began his story:

I was a youngster of about sixteen back in eighteen fifty-four. There wasn't a town of Comanche then. The only Comanche we knew were those redskins that rode their ponies like the devil himself. My pa thought I was old enough to do a man's work, and he took me on a scouting trip into this neck of Leon County. We weren't expecting trouble, but we kept on the lookout just in case. We's put out the fire and settled in when suddenly we was attacked by Comanches! You can just bet I was scared. I was so scared I just huddled down behind this tree thinking it was my

Martin Fleming and his Indian foes are history now, but the tree that saved his life still spreads its branches on the square in Comanche.

last night on this earth and I would be scalped alive. Somehow my pa fought them off, cause when dawn came we was both still alive. The trunk of this tree was filled with arrows, and I owe my life to it. I'm not going to let you cut it down without a fight.

With those defiant words, Mart took his stand squarely in front of his tree. The crowd murmured and buzzed with Uncle Mart's story. What harm could one tree do? Let it be. Humor the old man. He had earned his tree. And, to this day, the Fleming Oak stands on the square of Comanche, a living testimonial to a true Texas pioneer, Martin Fleming.

Mart led a varied life. His family moved from Georgia to Texas and settled in Bell County. When everyone else left the settlement with the advent of the Mexican War in 1845 the Flemings stayed and accepted an invitation from some Indians to live with the tribe. After two years with their red friends the Flemings began to fear the Indian influence on their son, and moved on.

Mart joined the Texas Rangers to fight on the frontier; he became a buffalo hunter, and finally he served with the Texas cavalry under General Forrest in the Civil War. Fleming received two wounds, a bullet in each leg. The one in his left leg he carried the rest of his life.

In 1872 Martin was back in Comanche to settle permanently on the land he and his father had surveyed eighteen years before. With his second wife, one daughter, and seven adopted children, the Ranger, soldier, and hunter became a stalwart citizen and one of the founders of the newspaper, *The Comanche Chief*.

As for that momentous day Uncle Mart saved his tree, even though the workmen may have thought he meant to use his shotgun, he later confessed, "I really meant my size ten boots." Regardless, Uncle Mart's tree lives on, and so does his memory.

What is rarely known is that this kind-hearted man felt his best accomplishments were helping young people secure an education or get a start in life. Even though not a church member himself, Martin Fleming helped educate several ministers for their calling. Fleming may be remembered best for saving a tree, but his unsung deeds of generosity helped settle the frontier he loved so much.

VI

Frontier Justice
and Mercy

The Littlest Ranger of Them All

Of all the valiant figures in Ranger annals, only Jones can be classified as a general. All the rest, including Hays, Ford, McCulloch, and McNelly were by comparison hardly more than rough and ready captains.

Walter Prescott Webb

**John B. Jones
Round Rock, 1878**

S AM BASS NEVER WENT down in outlaw annals as a successful thief. His best haul was $1,280, and that had to be split four ways. Sam's fame rests more on his eluding capture rather than on his ill-gotten gains. Cove Hollow was the outlaw's unpenetrable refuge, and when Sam met his doom, it was only through betrayal, by his cohort Jim Murphy.

Arrested for harboring criminals, Jim was told that if he helped the Rangers capture Bass he would go free. The traitor joined Bass at a time when hands were sorely needed, as Sam had started a new venture—bank robbery and the target was Round Rock. Poor Sam. He was fated to have even worse luck with banks. On the gang's way to the heist, Murphy managed to wire the Rangers. "We are on our way to Round Rock to rob the bank. For God's sake get there."

Though small of stature, John B. Jones was a man among men and the true hero of the legendary Texas Rangers.

The Rangers, under Captain John Jones, did get there before Bass and his pals arrived, but none of them were really prepared as three strangers casually rode into town late in the afternoon of July 19, 1878. Ranger Ware was in line for a shave and Major Jones was in the telegraph office.

As Bass and two accomplices, Barnes and Jackson, sauntered into Kopperel's store to case out the bank next door, two deputy lawmen, Grimes and Moore, accosted the trio. Major Jones had warned them to leave Bass to the Rangers, but Grimes foolishly demanded of Barnes, "Turn over that gun you're hiding!" Grimes never knew what hit him as Barnes killed him instantly. Moore tried to fire his gun, but with a blast from Barnes' gun his chest became a gaping hole.

The main street of Round Rock turned into a furious hailstorm of flying lead. The outlaws made a frantic dash for their horses, but a well-aimed bullet went through Barnes' head, and he fell dead at his horse's feet. Bass was hit hard and had to be helped on his horse by his true friend, Jackson. With bullets zinging past them, the pair made good their amazing escape. But, Sam Bass was a dying man. Frank Jackson finally heeded the pleas of his pal and left Sam to die alone.

Later that night a farmer came into town with the news that Sam was dying outside his cabin. The Rangers tried for three days to get Sam to name his confederates, but he refused. Finally with the words, 'The world's bobbling around," Sam Bass died on his twenty-seventh birthday. Jim Murphy got his comeuppance as well. In less than a year, some medicine meant for his eyes found its way into Jim's mouth, and the traitor died in convulsions.

It had taken Jones one hundred days to find Sam Bass, and only then with the aid of an informer. John B. Jones cared nothing about the notoriety that would follow for bringing the legendary Sam Bass to justice. He was a man who took tremendous pride in his profession of being a Texas Ranger, and Jones always got his man.

When you think of a heroic breed of men, the Texas Rangers fit every category. Relentless, brave, persevering, courageous, undaunted, and resourceful, these defenders of justice on the Texas frontier created some of the Lone State State's most colorful and exciting sagas of the Old West. Volumes have been written lauding the exploits of this dedicated group of men. But, one Ranger that never seemed to make the big time was actually "one of the most dangerous men to criminals that ever lived," John B. Jones.

After the Civil War the frontier and Mexican border became hotbeds of bandits, gunslingers, rustlers, marauding Indians, and every other thieving type opposed to law and order. Finally, in 1874 Governor Richard B. Coke passed a bill creating six companies of Rangers to be known as the Frontier Battalion. But, where was the frontier? It stretched for thousands of miles westward, and it would require incredible stamina on the part of the Batallion to patrol this vast territory. At their command was John B. Jones.

If you think of Texas Rangers as all John Wayne look-alikes, then you are wrong, for one of the greatest Rangers of them all was a slight man barely 5 feet 8 inches tall and weighing a mere 135 pounds. Always well dressed, mannerly, and a true gentleman, Jones was still as tough as they come. His men were treated equally and fairly, and he accepted the same conditions on the trail as his Rangers. No special considerations were given, and none were ever asked. In an era when men were renowned for being able to hold large quantities of hard liquor, Jones only drank black coffee or buttermilk. Major Jones may have been of small stature, but his men and his superiors thought of him as a giant among lawmen.

John grew up near Corsicana with an intense love of horses and was considered to be the equal of even the superb horsemen, the Comanches. His contemporaries stated that, "he was simply irresistible on horseback." During the Civil War Jones served with Terry's Texas Rangers, and within one month Private Jones became Captain Jones. He was the perfect choice of Governor Coke for the Frontier Battalion.

Jones' feats with his six companies of seventy-five men each were legion. Their first task was to subdue the marauding Indians. Moving fast, the Texans engaged the savages in fifteen fights, and by the middle of 1875 the Plains Indians were on the run. In one battle with the Kiowas against the wily Chief Lone Wolf, Jones and his small band were greatly outnumbered and trapped in a ravine. A cool-headed Jones rallied his men and managed to withstand the attacks. Lone Wolf's horse was shot, and the furious chief ordered the Rangers' mounts killed. Still the white men held out, repelling the redskins' charges. As night fell, only one ranger had been killed in an attempted escape to find aid. The Rangers were without water, food, or extra ammunition, and the Indians could have soon massacred them. However, during the night the Indians mysteriously vanished. Jones promptly marched his men to camp, mounted fresh horses, and started after the savages again.

With the end of the Indian menace, Jones turned his attention to the hundreds of fugitives from the law that made the Texas frontier their domain. This tireless Ranger cleaned up the notorious Kimble County (a haven for criminals) with forty-one arrests made without bloodshed. The criminals were chained to trees, as there was no jail or courtroom, and court was held and sentences carried out.

To settle the "Hoodoo War," which was nothing more than a feud between the German settlers of Mason County and the Anglos, Governor Coke dispatched John B. Jones. With utmost diplomacy on the part of Jones, the flames of the feud died. The same methods worked for Jones in the Horrell-Higgins feud in Lampasas. Jones just arrested them all and got each side to sign a peace treaty. Amazingly, each side honored the treaty, and the feud died out.

Jones' next big task was the confusing issues involved in the 1877 Salt War out in El Paso, 400 miles from the nearest Texas settlement. For generations, poor men from both sides of the Rio Grande had worked the natural salt deposits. Then, Texas granted the mineral rights on the land to their owners. A district judge, Charles Howard, refused to allow his land to be mined for the salt. The Mexicans revolted, captured Howard, and forced him to surrender his claim and leave town. Howard left, but only for a few days. He returned to shoot Don Louis Cardis, who he blamed for his troubles. Riots were resumed, and the governor sent John B. Jones to handle the explosive situation.

Jones went to El Paso alone. With his persuasive skill he got Howard to surrender for trial. Then the Ranger made a big mistake. Jones sent for Company C of his Battalion and placed John B. Tays in command. Tays was not the man for the job and trouble started immediately after Jones' departure. Howard got a new injunction to get his land back and set out with Tays and the Rangers to enforce his claim.

Legally, Howard was within the law, but he knew he was just stirring up trouble. The mob rallied again, surrounded the Rangers, and forced the inept Tays to surrender the helpless Howard. It was the only time a Ranger force was ever defeated. Howard was put before a firing squad and his body mutilated. The murder was a black mark against Tays.

Jones returned to El Paso and the issue of the Salt War was settled peaceably. No one was arrested, but there were no more attempts to mine the salt deposits either. It was only four months before Jones would serve his last field encounter—the capture and death of Sam Bass.

John B. Jones' exploits may not have been the stuff of legends that Hays, Ford, and McNelly created, but the smallest Ranger of them all with his use of diplomacy and tact was truly one of the force's superior commanders and an unsurpassed leader of men.

The Lead-Slug Necklace

**Dr. Sofie Herzog
Brazoria, 1905**

W HILE MOST LADIES WOULD rather be adorned with jewels, Dr. Sofie Herzog preferred her necklace made of bullets—those she had removed from her patients. She considered those twenty-four lead slugs as sort of a unique talisman. But, then Dr. Sofie Herzog was herself unique.

In an era when women were only expected to be housewives and to raise children, Dr. Sofie Herzog was daring indeed. Years ahead of her time, Dr. Sofie cut her hair (scandalous!), rode astride a horse, and would accept any challenge that added zest and adventure to her already exciting life. Yet, Sofie was still traditional in some respects: She married at fourteen and had fourteen children.

Medicine had always been a part of Sofie's life. Her father was an internationally known surgeon, and she married a young surgeon. With such a medical environment, Sofie decided to study medicine, too. As a wife and mother of fourteen Sofie must have been a brilliant student to have taken on the strict and rigorous demands of medical school. She was fortunate to have been born and raised in Austria, for being admitted to medical school in the United States during that backward era was almost impossible.

As fate would have it, in 1886 Sofie's husband accepted a job in New York. His decision would have a profound effect on his wife's career. The couple expected great things in their new life so far from Austria, but Sofie's husband died. This left Sofie, a middle-aged woman with numerous children all alone in a strange country. What could she do? Even though Sofie was a trained physician, women were not expected to have a profession, particularly that of a doctor. Women were much too delicate for such demanding work. In spite of all the prejudices against women in her chosen field, Sofie gained an excellent reputation and a devoted practice.

Then Sofie's youngest daughter decided to get married and move to Texas. As Sofie thought about her daughter's future as a pioneer in Texas, the challenge became more and more appealing to her. Her children were grown, and at forty-five, she thought, there might be some excitement for her as well in that wild land far to the south.

When the new doctor arrived in her new home in Texas, Brazoria was shocked. Not only was she female (gasp!), but she had *short* hair!

Sofie's patients were bandits, gunslingers, feuders, and squabbling pioneers, and the most common ailment she treated was gunshot wounds. Life was exciting indeed, and the refined world of New York and Vienna were forgotten. The frontier was where life was to be lived.

Civilization was ready to tame Sofie's frontier. In 1905 the St. Louis, Brownsville, and Mexican Railroad Company began laying tracks to Brazoria. With the railroad came accidents—serious accidents. A full-time doctor was a necessity. The dedicated Sofie found herself constantly on her horse out in the brush looking for the crew and the latest casualty. She decided that if she was going to spend all of her time treating railroad workers, she should get paid for it. So, in 1907 Sofie applied for the job as the railroad's chief surgeon. She was hired immediately by the railroad on the mistaken assumption that she was a man. Her reputation was impeccable, but when the board realized their error, they demanded she resign immediately.

Sofie refused, and told them, "If I fail, you can fire me." The board relented, and Sofie didn't fail. This indomitable doctor rode the rails anyway she could—in a box car, a passenger car, or the engine. It was not unusual to see a railroad worker frantically pumping a handcar down the track with Sofie clutching her hat and bag, urging him, "Faster! Faster!"

It wasn't easy, and it took time, but Sofie became a treasured member of Brazoria's society. Maybe it was the Episcopal Church she built, or the new hotel she financed, or maybe it was because they realized Sofie was truly a wonderful person.

Sofie did marry again. At age sixty-five the doctor became Mrs. Marion Huntington, the wife of a seventy-year-old plantation owner. No, Sofie did not settle down in her older years. She bought one of those rip-snorting, fire-breathing automobiles and drove eleven miles to work at her office for eleven more years.

In 1925 when Sofie was seventy-six years old, she finally quit her medical career—she died. Sofie had been a truly liberated woman! She had defied convention in every phase of her life to do what she knew was right. It must have been very hard to persevere against so much prejudice, but Sofie's story is the story of all heroes and heroines who against all odds followed their own convictions.

The Last Train Robbery

David Andrew
Trousdale
Sanderson, 1912

"WEST OF THE PECOS!" sounds like the title of a Hollywood western, but it's that arid and desolate land in southwest Texas that was so familiar to outlaws and gunslingers of Judge Roy Bean's day. With its raw terrain, hidden canyons, and close proximity to Mexico, this last frontier of Texas was the refuge of thieves, bandits, and murderers.

When the Silver Spike was driven on the southern route of the Southern Pacific in January of 1883 just west of the Pecos River, the railroad did bring civilization. It also brought men who would rather steal than grub out an honest existence in that hostile land.

One particular stretch of track trainmen hated was through the rugged desolation between Del Rio and Sanderson. Its isolation and numerous hideouts made it perfect country for a holdup. The Sunset Route did rate high on train robbers' itineraries. Even Black Jack Ketchum's gang carried off $6,000 in loot. Finally, on March 13, 1912, the last great train robbery on the Southern Pacific was foiled by a fast-thinking Wells Fargo agent, David Andrew Trousdale.

The desert was cold and dark on the night of March 12, and it was very late when Engine 709 pulled into Dryden. It was quite easy for the two masked men to climb aboard, stick a gun in the ribs of Engineer Grosh and Fireman Holmes, and order them to stop just up the tracks at Baxter's Curve. The masks hid Ben Kilpatrick, "The Tall Texan" of the Wild Bunch led by Butch Cassidy and the Sundance Kid, and Frank Hobeck. Kilpatrick and Hobeck had met in prison, and long enforced confinement had not convinced either of the ex-cons that crime does not pay.

Guarding the Wells Fargo shipment was messenger Trousdale, totally unaware of the trouble up in the engine. When asked to open the baggage

compartment by the trainmen, the messenger found himself facing an armed masked man. It was Frank Hobeck or "Ole Beck," as he was called. The thief lined up the crew, frisked them, and had the engine and mail cars uncoupled from the coaches. The bandits and the working part of the train chugged about a mile down the tracks leaving the passengers marooned in the desert.

Everything was going according to plan as Kilpatrick stayed with the engine and Hobeck forced Trousdale and his helper, Reagan, back to the mail car. For some reason "Ole Beck" was unhappy and liberally cursed and threatened the Wells Fargo agents. Trousdale realized he was powerless unless he could catch Hobeck off guard.

Feigning cowardice, Trousdale began to gripe sullenly about his poor salary and how Wells Fargo didn't pay him enough to fight. As far as he was concerned the company deserved to be robbed. The messenger kept on with his bitter complaining, and Hobeck stopped cursing and began to listen to the whining man. Trousdale even began to helpfully point out things about the car and became a fellow conspirator with the thief. Trousdale had found his opportunity to "get even" with Wells Fargo for treating him so poorly.

Ole Beck must have been far from bright, for he failed to see the agent slip a large ice maul under his coat. Nor was Hobeck suspicious when the clever dissembler pointed out a package that probably held something of value. Trousdale had done such a good job of fooling the bandit that Hobeck became so fascinated with the promise of loot, he leaned his rifle against the side of the railroad car. Hobeck even bent over and turned his back on his captive! What an opportunity! And, Trousdale took it! What few brains Frank Hobeck had spilled over the baggage car! Now to take care of Kilpatrick!

Trousdale gave Reagan and the mail clerk, Bank, each one of Hobeck's pistols. He kept the Winchester, and they settled down to wait. They waited, and waited, and waited. Still no Kilpatrick. What was keeping him? In exasperation Trousdale finally fired a shot through the roof of the car. Ben took his own sweet time about finding out what the problem was, but finally Trousdale heard, "Frank? Frank?" By now, the Wells Fargo man was about to lose his sanity, and the waiting had put his nerves on a raw edge. At last Kilpatrick's curiosity got the best of him, and the Tall Texan stuck his head around the door. The robber never knew what hit him. With amazing aim, Trousdale killed him with a single shot. The bullet went in Kilpatrick's left eye, out the back of his head and into the wall of the baggage car.

At 5 a.m. the Southern Pacific was on its way once more. Kilpatrick had been carrying six sticks of dynamite and Hobeck a bottle of nitroglycerine. Their bodies were unloaded at Sanderson, propped up and grisly photographs taken. Trousdale was a hero. Large rewards for service in the line of duty were not the usual policy for Wells Fargo, but Trousdale was given $1,000. Also, the Southern Pacific added $500 to that reward and the grateful passengers donated a gold medal.

Friday, March 13, 1912, was truly an unlucky day for Ben Kilpatrick and Frank Hobeck, but luckily for the Southern Pacific, with their demise the era of train robbery ended on the Sunset Route.

No Night Too Dark

PERHAPS THE REAL HERO, or heroine in this case, of the story of
Dr. Doss is Mildred Patterson. Pioneer days are rich with stories
of primitive medicines and treatments, but most of these early
doctors died as forgotten as their patients. Mildred Patterson wanted the
memory of her community's beloved Dr. Doss preserved. In order to ac-
complish this, Mildred took it upon herself to see that a monument to Dr.
Doss was erected.

**Dr. Edward D. Doss
Bend, 1925**

This innovative lady sent letters to Doss's relatives and put her story in
the paper. Hundreds of the doctor's patients remembered his kindness
and sent Mildred donations. In less than two months there was enough
money for the monument. As Mildred said, "Probably a lot of people
sent money who had never paid him and now wanted to make amends."

On the simple monument is a picture of Dr. Doss and his faithful horse,
Ross. Doss and Ross must have been quite a team for his practice took in
Bend, Chapel, Rough Creek, Colony, and Nix. People nearly always got
sick at night, so when the tired doctor would get back in his buggy after a
late call, he could doze off, for he knew Ross would bring him safely
home.

Back in those days doctors had to treat a raft of diseases that have now
all but disappeared. There were epidemics of cholera, yellow fever, ty-
phoid, smallpox, malaria, scarlet fever, diphtheria, and polio. A lot of
bleeding and purging was done, and quinine and calomel were given in
heroic doses. Sulphur and molasses and sassafras tea were good old stand-

Pioneer Dr. Doss and his
faithful horse Ross were
an unbeatable team for
frontier medicine.

bys as well. It is no wonder patent medicines liberally laced with alcohol were so popular.

Mildred's memories of Dr. Doss are sketchy, but she did recall that he told all the children he brought the babies in his black bag. Then, Mildred said, "He would throw back his head and laugh. I can still see his long white beard sticking straight out in front of him."

Dr. Doss ran a country store, clinic, hospital, and office all in one building. He probably had the store out of necessity to make ends meet, as most doctors in those days were paid in farm goods—if at all. Mildred said, "It was the largest store Bend ever had. In the back Dr. Doss mixed his medicines and saw patients. I remember a great big chair, because he was also the dentist. He had a large room where he brought sick people that needed special attention, and he kept them several days or even weeks."

At the dedication of the monument in May of 1965 these words were spoken: "Dr. Doss was a man who found no night too dark and cold or no road too long and muddy to answer the call to help his fellowman."

There are probably hundreds of dedicated pioneer doctors who deserve this accolade as well as Dr. Doss, and it is sad there are so few Mildred Pattersons who make it their contribution to history to see that their memories endure.

VII
Heroes of the Oil Patch

Rescue Beneath the Earth

The Old-Timer
Breckenridge, 1920

I N THE FRENZIED DAYS of the big oil strikes, wildcatters would drill for the black gold under Texas soil wherever they thought a well would come in. City streets were lined with derricks and houses and buildings moved if there was even the slightest chance of finding oil. Nothing else was important. Just bringing in a producing well was all that seemed to matter, and, hard tough men were needed for this backbreaking work.

It was noon on a hot summer day in the booming town of Breckenridge. Tired hungry men broke for lunch and left their well unattended. A deep hole had been drilled, but no pipe had been set. The young housewife in the small cottage next to the well was busy preparing a simple lunch when to her horror she missed her baby who had been crawling happily under her feet. The frantic mother ran outside crying for her baby, but the toddler wasn't to be found. When her husband arrived the mother was almost in hysterics. The only place her baby could be was at the bottom of the well hole, and probably dead.

The well crew had returned and these experienced men knew there was only one thing to do. The driller said, "We gotta lower a man in the hole."

"Let me go," the distraught father demanded.

"You're too big. I'd go myself but I'd never get down there without the sides of the hole caving in and burying me and your son."

The tooldresser and roustabout wanted to go, but the driller said, "It'll have to be a slim tough guy, mighty thin and mighty tough."

The crowd dispersed to find a brave man willing to risk his life many feet beneath the earth. In a little while the driller returned with a slight, weatherbeaten middle-aged man with a determined set to his jaw. A rope was tied around his skinny waist, and he was slowly lowered into the abyss.

The suspense was tremendous. Would he find the baby? Would the little boy be alive? Would they both be buried by a cave-in, or would they survive their perilous ascent? The wait was agonizing. The parents were in the throes of anguish and the crowd had their heart in their throat.

Slowly the well crew let the rope out waiting anxiously for the tug signaling them to stop. Down the man went, farther and farther. How the man could even see in such a narrow slot was beyond comprehension. Suddenly, two tugs on the rope! Pull him up! But carefully! The walls of the hole could still come crumbling down!

After an eternity the old-timer's head appeared out of the hole. As his shoulders surfaced, the crowd could see that in his arms was the baby, still alive and unhurt. The mother almost fainted with joy. The father laughed and cried at the same time, and even the tough, hardened workers felt a tear in their eye. Such a miracle was amazing. Finally, the grateful parents turned to shower the man who had saved their baby with thanks. But, he was gone. The old-timer had disappeared. In all of the excitement the unknown hero had slipped away. No one would ever know his name, but a thankful mother and father would remember him forever.

"Let Me to Thy Bosom Fly"

Bill the Shooter Breckenridge, 1920

A SHOOTER, BACK IN the roaring boomdays of oil exploration, could figure on working about three years. If in that time he hadn't been blown to bits "shooting" a well, he had had such a close call he changed professions.

Shooting a well was done after a test well was drilled and little or no oil struck. Nitroglycerin was set off at the bottom of the hole and the explosion ripped rock formations to shreds, so that if oil was trapped in the crevices, the shock would cause it to flow. Too often the worker who fired the well was blown to bits along with the rock.

One such recalcitrant well had been drilled in a vacant lot next to a church in the boomtown of Breckenridge. Even though the oil flowed in spurts, the experts felt a shot of nitro would make it a gusher. The best shooter in the business was called in.

Bill was about thirty, swaggering, loud, and profane. He liked a fight, a poker game, and the bright lights of the dance halls. Needless to say, Bill was often in company with the boomtown's soiled doves. Broad shouldered and square jawed, Bill's face was always red from the wind and sun and probably hootch as well. In his khaki pants and shirt, battered wide brimmed hat, and mud-encrusted leatherlace boots, Bill was the perfect example of Joe Roughneck, the symbol of all oil patch workers.

Why they picked a Sunday morning to shoot this particular well, no one knows. Perhaps it was because the well was quiet and not spurting one of its irregular flows of oil. Bill and his helper packed their innocent-looking tin containers, each holding ten quarts of nitroglycerin, in a rubber-lined compartment in their bright red truck marked "Danger: Explosives!" and headed for their perilous task.

Other drivers on that rough, rutted road hastily pulled over the instant they spied that familiar red truck. With a prayer on their lips, motorists waited with clenched knuckles until Bill bounced past on his dangerous ride.

When Bill and his helper, who had to be very brave as well, reached the stubborn well, they poured the contents of two cans of the volatile liquid into a long slim tin shell that resembled a piece of gutter pipe. They would then place all the shells they filled one on top of the other in a vertical line at the bottom of the hole for firing.

When the first shell was filled with twenty quarts of nitro, Bill held it aloft while his assistant took a soft cloth and gently wiped the outside. The shell had to be lowered 3,000 feet through the casing, and if one single drop of nitro on the outside of the shell came in contact with the casing, the friction could blow them all to kingdom come. No doubt only Bill and his helper were on the drilling rig when this delicate job was done. It's hard to imagine a bunch of wide-eyed spectators hovering over a shooter's shoulder.

While the shell was being lowered, as fate would have it, the ground began to shake and there was a deep roar beneath the casing. The spasmodic well was beginning another of its irregular flows. When the shell hit this huge spurt of crude, it would be lifted out of the hole, hit the derrick and blow up the rig as well as everyone near at hand. Not only that, the explosion would set off the store of nitro in the truck and a far more powerful blast would wipe out everything for hundreds of yards.

Without waiting for Bill's wild yell of "Run for your lives!" his helper and the crew raced frantically for safety with Bill only a few feet behind them. The shooter had run only a few yards when he heard the organ and congregation of the small rural church raise their voices in song:

> Jesus, Lover of my soul,
> Let me to Thy bosom fly,
> While the nearer waters roll,
> While the tempest still is high.

Little did the worshipers realize how close they actually were to flying to that bosom. But Bill knew! The scene of bodies buried under piles of rubble, the anguished cries, the untimely deaths flashed before him. That shell must be stopped!

Perhaps without realizing what he was doing, in one magnificent gesture of heroism Bill the Shooter rushed back to the well. Crouching beside the hole, he waited for that silver piece of tin to erupt from its interrupted burial ground. With eyes and throat burning from the oil and gas, Bill grasped at the shell as it rose on its cushion of crude and mud. So slick and slimy was the metal, the shell almost slipped from his grasp. Miraculously, Bill the Shooter managed to hold on to the missile of twenty quarts of canned nitro until the stunned workers ran up and relieved him of the ominous burden.

The small church never knew how close they came to the Valley of Death. Seconds later there was another mighty roar. A gusher! And without the nitro! As for Bill the Shooter, true to his profession, he finished his job with, "Boys, let's have a drink!"

"More Beef But Less Beefing"

DURING THOSE EARLY DEPRESSION years when thousands came seeking the wealth trapped under the East Texas soil and rock, many left as poor as they arrived. In contrast to their stories of disillusionment and failure, is the comic relief provided by the success story of "Governor" Willie.

No one remembers his last name, he was just known as Oil Field Willie who followed the boomtowns. When Willie arrived in Kilgore, he not only found one of the biggest booms in the United States, he found a title and a final resting place.

Willie was not exactly the village idiot, but he was the town character with a special affinity for politics. Kilgore had suddenly found itself with thousands of inhabitants and was forced to incorporate. The leading merchant, Malcolm Crim, was elected mayor on his promises of modern improvements for Kilgore.

It was about this time that Willie made his appearance in town and took it upon himself to comment on the muddy conditions of the streets. For a man who should have been used to muddy streets by now, it was comical to see Willie on a soap box attracting a crowd as he harangued his audience about mud. A heavy-set man smoking a pipe was in Willie's audience and asked a bystander, "Who's the fellow who doesn't like our streets?"

"Governor" Willie Kilgore, 1935

"Governor" Willie became a wonderful and beloved comic relief during those frenzied boom days in the East Texas oil fields.

"Oh, just some nut," was the answer.

"Well, he doesn't sound nutty to me," replied Malcom Crim, "I don't like mud either, and I'm the mayor."

No matter how Willie felt about mud, the police had their own feelings about a man with no visible means of support. When the police picked him up, Willie was told he would have to work out a fine by picking peas at the county farm. Willie's reaction was, "I didn't plant them peas; I don't eat peas and so, as shore as hell, I'm not goin' to pick any damn peas!" The police laughed and turned him loose. Willie's antics and wisecracks make for some colorful stories.

Back in those days you could buy hootch in Louisiana but not in Texas. Naturally, many Texas residents crossed over the state line for their entertainment. When some wit suggested to Willie, "Why don't you run?," Willie replied,

"All right, but for what?"

"Run for the state line," was the facetious answer.

The next thing Kilgore knew Willie was handing out campaign cards announcing, "I'm running for the state line."

Soon Willie was such a favorite with everyone in Kilgore and a town "institution," he was proclaimed "Governor of the East Texas Oil Field" and was always introduced by his honorable title.

Willie could neither read nor write, a fact well known around Kilgore. When someone handed him a letter, Willie's stock remark was, "Well, what do you know about that!"

The "Governor" was welcome to walk into a cafe and eat a meal on the house, have a cigar at the drug store, and when he needed clothes, he charged them to Crim who always paid the account. One morning an oil field worker on his way to the well stopped at a cafe, put his dinner pail on the floor and was having a cup of coffee when Governor Willie entered. An argument developed and the worker said angrily, "You're stupid."

Willie retorted, "Maybe so, but you don't see me carrying no tin bucket."

A newly arrived panhandler asked a well-dressed man puffing a cigar for a dime. Governor Willie gestured with the cigar and growled, "Get over yonder; I'm working this side of the street."

When Willie announced that he was a candidate for "re-election" his candidacy was "subject to the action of the plutocratic primary" and his platform was to "Hiss Hitler; muzzle Mussolini."

Willie made a speech, and he was for "More oil well but less oil; more beef but less beefing; and more rain but less mud-slinging." Someone had Willie record his platform, and it was a bigger favorite on Kilgore's jukeboxes than "Pistol-Packin' Mama."

One sad night Willie was mortally injured in a car accident. Kilgore was disconsolate. Even though they had kidded their "Governor" unmercifully, they were genuinely fond of their buffoon who had provided so much amusement during those years of turmoil and hectic growth. The town honored their "governor" with a big funeral, and there wasn't a dry eye in the house. On his tombstone was engraved, "Governor Willie."

A Fellow Has Just One Time to Die

**Tex Thornton
Amarillo, 1948**

A S HUNGRY AS INSURANCE men were in those Depression years of the thirties, there wasn't a single one who would even try to sell Tex Thornton a life insurance policy. Tex had the kind of job very few would relish, even in those dark days when men were desperate for work. Tex Thornton was an oil well firefighter, and the tools of his dangerous trade were quarts of nitroglycerin.

The scourge of the oil field is a well fire. Not only do millions of dollars go up in a blazing inferno, the danger spreads to other wells, and workers are in mortal peril. But, the fires can be put out by someone with incredible nerve, so when a well went wild, someone was certain to say, "You better call Tex Thornton."

Thornton was a true professional in every sense of the word. He was as devoted to nitro and its destructiveness as any scientist. A few miles out of Amarillo Thornton set up his own factory, manufactured his own explosives, and mixed his own chemicals in marble vats. Usually Tex mixed enough to last two or three months for there was at least one fire every month and sometimes as many as four. Fires could start from lightning, friction during drilling, hot boilers, or hot iron. Gas could travel along the ground to a boiler as far as one hundred feet away, ignite, and shoot like a rocket back to the well from which it came.

It took one to four days to put out a fire, but Tex had been extremely lucky and extinguished one real blazer in two hours and forty minutes. As Tex said,

> Most of the time in fighting a fire is spent in preparation. There is water to pump and wreckage to move. Red hot iron will ignite the well again even after the fire is extinguished, so all iron must be moved. It's not the easiest thing in the world to clean away the debris. In putting out a fire I generally take two, twenty-foot posts and place them on opposite sides of the well about one-hundred-eighty feet apart. An asbestos belt runs from one to the other right by the well. On this belt I slide the shells containing the explosives to the fire and leave them. Then I go to the post from which I started, and by means of a pulley swing the shells into the fire at the moment I set them off by electricity by pressing a button with my foot. The force of the explosion is so much greater than the force of the gas that the fire is blown out in the same manner that you blow out a candle.

Thornton was not a fatalist. He stayed alive because he was cautious and careful. The firefighter's nerves of steel are evident in this story where Tex tells of the fire in Powell, New Mexico:

> The oil had flowed over everything. It seemed as if the whole earth was on fire. For three hundred yards, a nearby creek was a raging sea of flame. The fire

Tex Thornton was a man
who knew and respected
nitroglycerin, both its
blessings and its awesome
destructiveness.

around the well had to be put out first before I could get near the well itself. I used five shots in the creek itself, stringing them at intervals of one hundred yards each. They were dropped through the fire, and into the water, to the bottom of the creek. Then wires extending from my switch were attached to them—one for each shot. At each explosion water, dirt, fire, oil, shot in every direction. Every window pane in Powell was broken, but the fire was extinguished.

Tex made putting out oil field fires sound easy, but he did admit that some wells were difficult.

Once two thousand people gathered to watch me. The company, rather than disappoint them, had me shoot the well quite before I was ready. Because the asbestos belt was too slack, the first shot was carried in by the fire and thrown off to one side where it exploded. The same thing happened the next time. The third time I got the fire out, but it caught again from some hot irons fifty feet away. I saw the fire flash like a bolt of lightning to the well, and I tried another shot. This time the fire was out for good.

This great firefighter was born in 1892 near Oxford, Mississippi. About 1913 Tex went to Cleveland, Ohio, where he became an expert student with a company that taught the proper use of explosives. The next stop was the oil fields of West Texas to test his skills. Muscular and strong, the man had nerve without being foolhardy, and was brave without being boastful. He loved people, and like Will Rogers, Tex never met a stranger and had a host of friends.

Tex was introduced to the Panhandle in 1920 when hired by the Knox Oil Company. Although he never showed a fear of nitro, Tex was aware he was surely courting danger and once remarked, "A fellow has just one time to die. I do believe it can be hurried along a little by recklessness or carelessness."

No, Tex was not betrayed by the nitro he handled so well. He was mysteriously beaten on the head and garroted with his own shirt in a motel room in Amarillo. The murder in 1948 rocked the Panhandle. Not even World War II received the coverage of this sensational murder. Tex had picked up a man and woman hitchhiking out of Tucumcari, New Mexico. The three checked into a motel in Amarillo, and the couple left the next day driving Tex's car. From all appearances it looked as though the unknown couple were guilty of the brutal murder. Tex was known to carry huge sums of money, particularly after finishing a job, as he had on this occasion. When the hitchhikers turned themselves in, they were acquitted of the crime. Whoever extinguished the life of Tex Thornton is still unknown.

Tex's contribution to the oil industry is inestimable. Many companies might have ended in bankruptcy but for this firefighter's skill. Not only was he an expert in his hazardous profession, he was a pioneer in the field of fighting oil well fires. As his biographer, F. Stanley, put it, "Whenever a hall of fame is built by the oil industry, Tex Thornton will undoubtedly have an outstanding place among the heroes of the business."

VIII
Visionaries, Missionaries, and Entrepreneurs

The Children Nobody Wanted

**Louisa Ervendberg
New Braunfels,
1846**

T HE JOURNEY HAD BEEN one long *Leichenzug*—a funeral procession. Their dead reached from the port of Indianola to their final graveyard in New Braunfels. This second wave of more than 5,000 German immigrants arrived in Texas during the early part of 1846, and awaiting them was only disease and starvation.

This was a different Texas from the Republic that had greeted Prince Solms and his band the previous year. Texas was a state now and once again at war with her arch enemy Mexico. Every available wagon and team had been commandeered for transporting troops to the border. No one cared about 5,000 foreigners stranded on the Texas beach. Conditions were so ghastly and deplorable that many Germans died without ever seeing the land of milk and honey promised them in New Braunfels.

Finally in sheer desperation to escape the horrors of their rude encampment, many families began to walk inland to their new home. Totally unprepared for the vastness of their new land, the long murderous trek was littered with cherished personal belongings. Also lining the trail were heartbreaking graves, many of them very small.

To further add to the sad plight of the pitiful band, the Guadalupe River was at flood, and they were unable to reach the colony. It was unbearably hot that dreadful July, and when they were able to cross the river, another disaster struck. Fever! The word was feared as much as "Indians!" Both were equally as deadly, and the church records for that terrible year show 304 deaths within the parish. There was very little that

could be done for these new settlers, but the most tireless and devoted workers to aid them were John O. Meusebach and the Reverend Louis Ervendberg and his devoted wife, Louisa.

Louisa had already proved she was made of the stuff of a true pioneer woman. When she married the young Louis Ervendberg in Chicago, she had followed him willingly to the frontier of the Republic of Texas. Land was cheap, and ministers were few.

When they finally settled in the community of Blumenthal in Colorado County, they had buried two babies and now had a dear little girl. The minister did well with his flock, but Ervendberg was a man who always looked to greener pastures, and Louisa was the kind of wife who would accompany him.

In 1844 a group of German nobles known as the *Adelsverein* were financing a colony on a tract of land northwest of San Antonio. They contacted Ervendberg and offered the minister the pastorate of this new German settlement. It was too good for Louis to turn down.

When Louis went to meet his new congregation when they landed at Lavaca Bay, Louisa stayed behind in Blumenthal to await her fourth baby. When spring arrived she set out to meet her husband and the immigrants at the site of the new settlement on the Guadalupe River. This amazing woman was alone in an unknown land. Not only did she have her new baby son and young daughter to care for, she had to see to the horses and the milk cows tied behind her wagon. After weeks of slow, grueling travel Louisa reached the Guadalupe River, but no one was there. Louisa Ervendberg was the first German woman to see the site of New Braunfels. Here, in a desolate land, miles from civilization, Louisa camped and waited—in the heart of Comanche territory. What stamina! What fortitude! Only a woman of amazing self control could have made such a hard journey only to find no one to welcome her.

Fortunately, it wasn't too long before the first contingent of German colonists arrived at their new home in Texas. Prince Carl with his Prussian soldiers looked terribly out of place on the Texas frontier. Not far behind was Louis, and the couple were reunited.

The Ervendberg's cabin was the first home to be built in New Braunfels, and it served as church and parsonage. For almost no wages, Louis preached on Sunday, taught school during the week, and in his spare time worked his fields and garden. Louisa gave of herself unsparingly as well. She shared her cows' milk and her vegetables with her neighbors and listened to the endless complaints from the women. Their European heavy garments were too hot for the unrelenting Texas heat, and they did not like the native food. Why, only pigs ate corn, they said. And, where was their staple *kartoffel,* the white potato? How could a decent *hausfrau* cook without potato soup, potato pancakes, and the mainstay of every German menu, boiled potatoes? Added to Louisa's woes was the death of the baby that had delayed her joining Louis in this Texas wilderness.

With the arrival of the new immigrants in that tragic summer of 1846, Louisa's and Louis' lives were irrevocably changed. When the fever epidemic finally subsided, the grisly death count was made and sixty newly orphaned children were homeless in a hostile land. Relatives and friends adopted most of the poor forlorn waifs, but there were still nineteen children remaining without any place to go. There was no one to take care of them but Pastor and Mrs. Ervendberg. What a heroic decision! Large families were certainly not unusual on the frontier, but having nineteen extra mouths to feed was somewhat overwhelming.

The little church and parsonage had to be abandoned for the Ervendberg's large new family. Louis finally obtained land north of New Braunfels that they named "New Wied," and in 1848 the West Texas Orphan Asylum, the first in the state, was incorporated. *Wiesenfarm* was a large frame house, neither completely German, nor completely Texan, but it provided a happy and bountiful home at New Wied for those first years.

Every hand was constantly busy. Louis taught school and preached and was an avid amateur botanist. He experimented in Egyptian cotton, wheat from North Africa, silk worms, and tobacco. There was corn to be harvested, cows to be milked, pigs to be fed and made into fat German sausages, and vegetables to be raised to feed growing bodies. New Wied became almost self-supporting.

Louisa was the perfect example of the aphorism "a woman's work is never done." She and her girls including her own three daughters baked more than twenty loaves of bread everyday. With only three Dutch ovens, each holding only one loaf, it was an arduous task. But that was only to start the day. Not a minute was wasted by Louisa and her charges.

Christmas was an especially wonderful time at "New Wied." Louisa and her girls would be busy in the kitchen beginning in November. There was wine to be made from the wild mustang grapes, as well as plum and grape compote—and Christmas cookies! Aromatic odors would fill the house! There were gifts to be made for everyone, knitted caps for the boys and homemade aprons for the girls. For "Papa," there was a new volume from the Smithsonian Institute.

A magnificent cedar would be cut from the orphanage land and decorated with paper ornaments and cookies. The pungent scent of its branches would fill the schoolroom. Underneath a miniature city of Jerusalem with a tiny baby Jesus and hovering angel would be placed.

What a joyous occasion Christmas holidays were for the orphans. Louisa had created a home of warmth and love, not only for the now five children of her own, but for nineteen orphans who would always cherish those years at New Wied.

Louis Ervendberg was a man of a simple but beautiful character. He gave of himself to his flock, but people forgot the great services he had performed for them. The minister became bitter over his meager salary and resigned from his church. Then there was a very serious problem of one of the orphan girls. At seventeen she was the downfall of her pastor, protector, and teacher.

Louisa confronted her husband, and Louis promised to reject the young girl. If Louisa would take their three girls and return to Chicago, Louis would join her with their two young sons after closing the orphanage. They would open a school in the middle west together. Louisa returned to her old home and waited and waited for Louis and her children. She never saw him or her two sons again.

After realizing Louis was not going to join her, a saddened Louisa came back to New Braunfels, filed for divorce, and regained possession of the *Wiesenfarm*. It wasn't long before this indomitable woman married again, a man ten years younger named Balthazar Preiss. Louisa had two more children and the orphanage once again rang with laughter. But, after twenty-three years of marriage to Preiss, Louisa divorced him, claiming he was a man of an ungovernable temper. In an era when even one divorce was unthinkable, the uncompromising Louisa had two.

Louisa lived on at the orphanage with her children and grandchildren, but she never forgot her beloved Louis. She cherished his silver soup spoon and allowed no one else to use it. Years and years later it was discovered that Louis had been murdered by Mexican bandits in the small mining town where he had fled with the young orphan girl. By a strange quirk of fate the youngest daughter of Louis' second marriage met the oldest daughter of his first, and the mystery of Louis' fate was solved.

Louisa died during the Christmas season she loved so dearly, and she was buried on a cold Christmas Eve in 1887. Her great-grandchildren, the Timmermann sisters of Geronimo, still decorate for Christmas as Louisa did so many years ago. The green boughs are hung, a cedar tree is filled with cookies and the old-fashioned decorations, and the city of Jerusalem is placed lovingly under the tree. Louisa and her orphans are never forgotten.

A Lady with Visions

Martha White
McWhirter
Belton, 1866

YOU REALLY HAVE TO admire those Texas pioneer women. Life was a challenge even when nothing was happening. There were those lonely days of nothing but drudgery and toil from dawn far into the night. The sun turned their skin to leather, and hard working hands became cracked and broken. Babies died from lack of proper care, and a simple accident could result in death. To add to all of the other hardships of life on the frontier, there were marauding Indians. Women simply didn't have time to think of getting the vote, fighting for women's rights, and demanding to be treated equally. All that occupied most women was survival—that is except for Martha McWhirter.

It was a hot August evening as Martha McWhirter made her way home from a revival meeting. Life had not been easy with the death of her brother and two of her children. As she walked down the darkening street, suddenly a voice spoke to Martha: "Martha! It is time to take thought of your life and the evils around you!" Profoundly moved, all night Martha prayed and struggled. The next morning as she washed dishes, she experienced what she could only describe as a pentecostal baptism. The voice she had heard had been the voice of God, and she felt she was being called to do His work. Martha McWhiter had been sanctified!

Martha White McWhirter of Belton (seated second from left) led one of America's first liberated women's movement. All it took was visions.

Martha McWhirter never actually wrote down the tenets of sanctification, and it was only near the end of her life that she gave the three basic points for a magazine interview. First, sanctification came from God. You could pray for it, earnestly pray for it, but it only came to the worthy. Secondly, God made his wishes known through visions, dreams, and voices, and third, only the sanctified could interpret those visions. Unfortunately, God did not always speak to couples, and Mr. McWhirter never got the message. So, the sanctified partner should make every effort to keep their marriage happy and serene. However, living with a saint is not easy to do, so if the unbelieving spouse should cause trouble or leave, then the sanctified partner was no longer required to live with the unsanctified member. Regardless, the partner which was so blessed with sanctification kept the children. You can easily see how sanctification can cause all sorts of problems, particularly in those male chauvinistic days of 1866.

Martha was not to go through the rest of her life without a devoted following. She had already been a member of an interdenominational women's group that met one day a week. Their objective was to pray for guidance with their problems, and of course, most of the problems were caused by their husbands. Women were trapped in those days in a very real sense. They were unable to own property and often found themselves forced to beg their husband for money. Even enduring drunk husbands was not as degrading as having to beg for spending money.

Mrs. McWhirter told her fellow women about her hearing the voice of God and how she was sanctified. Naturally, the rest of the women prayed for sanctification as well. Martha told them how through dreams and visions she received God's advice on practical problems. What they could do to really help each other was pool what little money they had. Precious savings from hoarded funds were donated to the cause. One unmarried sister, brought her total savings of $20. Through bits and pieces the fund began to grow.

There is nothing in the world that gives more self-confidence than financial independence. Husbands, long accustomed to controlling their dutiful wives by the purse strings, began to feel the effects of the McWhirter planning. When they denied their wives a legitimate need, the sister merely had to go to group, explain her plight, and the money was there. Then, one day when one woman and her child had been brutalized by her drunken husband, she came for sanctuary at Mrs. McWhirter's home. Kind-hearted Mr. McWhirter let Sister Pratt work out her keep by helping Martha.

More money was always needed for the fund. None of the sisters minded hard work; they were used to that. They asked God for guidance. The answer came when one of the "Sancties's" neighbors needed laundry done. Of course they all prayed, and God advised it was proper for them to take in washing. One irate nasty husband caught the sisters doing the laundry in his house, and he put a gash in his wife's head. The three other women actually fought back. Somehow, *he* preferred charges, and the poor women had to pay him a hundred-dollar fine.

As the fund grew, so did the sisters' rights. Some began asking their husbands for wages. The McWhirter home was soon overrunning with sisters who had left their unhappy homes, now that they had a place to go and a way to earn money. Taking in laundry was better than living with a stingy dominating man. As for Mr. McWhirter, he finally moved out. Even though he never understood Martha's visions, he did understand kindness, and he never gave his wife any trouble for her beliefs and her work. He lived and died alone in his apartment over a store that he owned, and the town blamed Martha for his neglect.

Of course, the town split wide open over the rising number of Sancties. The only thing they agreed on was that it would never have happened if it hadn't been for Martha McWhirter, and the movement would last only as long as she did. Their main complaint was how she rigidly stood behind every woman that left their husband. Woman after woman found their way to the Sancties, and even though they were read out of their church, nothing would make them return to a miserable homelife. They merely became closer and continued to pray for guidance.

One night a furious husband demanded his wife back, and when she failed to appear, he sent a bullet through the door hoping to frighten her into returning home. But women who had taken abuse from the town, defied their church, and worked like slaves were not in the least afraid of a gun. The woman refused to leave, and the husband gave up in disgust.

There are wonderful stories about the Sancties. Two Dow brothers arrived in town from Scotland. They had been members of a sanctified group in their home country, and they asked Mrs. McWhirter for permission to join her group. The men of Belton were furious. Women joining was one thing, but for men to become Sanctificationists was too much. The poor Scotsmen were taken out and beaten and warned to leave town. When the brothers refused to go, they were tried for lunacy, and taken to the asylum in Austin. They only were "crazy" for one night and were released when the British Consul intervened. There is no proof, but you might hazard a guess as to who informed the Consul about the injustice towards the Dows.

Another incident of "insanity" occurred when a widow Johnson was left a large life insurance policy by her unsanctified husband. A greedy brother-in-law had her committed to the asylum where she became a seamstress. Martha and her sisters did their usual prayer routine, and God advised them to write the governor. It wasn't long before Governor

Ireland had Sister Johnson back among the fold, not only with her life insurance policy but with the ninety dollars she earned in the asylum as well.

Belton may not have approved of the Sanctificationists, but the ladies were slowly but surely amassing a tidy sum of money in their fund. Some were nurses, some were cooks, and a few even cut cedar posts and sold them for firewood. There was no limit as to what the women would do rather than return to their bullying husbands. However, the big money maker for the sisters was their hotel. One of the widows had inherited a big rambling and rather dilapidated hotel which she donated to the fund. It wasn't long before word got around about the hotel's clean rooms and good fresh food. The enterprising sisters had also installed a steam laundry that not only did the hotel laundry, but took in the townspeople's wash as well.

The hotel business proved so lucrative, that when Mrs. McWhirter asked God's advice on building a new one, He readily agreed. The Central Hotel was a big unadorned three-story affair that was clean and comfortable and served the best food in the state. Travelers couldn't get there fast enough. Workers rotated their duties, so the waitresses one week might be the cooks the next. That way, no one complained about allocation of duties.

A Professor Garrison reported that the sisters still relied on dreams and their daily prayer meetings, but they had become so close, that ideas seemed to come to all of them rather than just one seeing "The Way." He also deduced that economic necessity probably had a predominance over religious fervor.

The sisters wore plain dark clothes that were out of style, but all were exceptionally neat and tidy. Not only had one of the women become an excellent dentist, but another became an expert cobbler. Martha McWhirter certainly had no objections to men joining her group, but none seemed cut out for their lifestyle. Nor did she have any objections to employing men, and several worked at the hotel and laundry. The sisters fared so well in the hotel business, they leased two more in Waco and turned a tidy profit on them.

When the sisterhood could afford a vacation, they did it up in style. Martha rented a house in New York for the summer of 1880. The entire group, in three divisions, spent six weeks taking in the sights of the big city. They traveled up by rail and returned by boat, docking at Galveston. You can bet they would have never gotten a trip like that if they had stayed with their husbands. Even Belton was beginning to come around and admit the sisters were admirable. It didn't hurt when the town found out George McWhirter had left his Martha a handsome estate and even made her the executrix of his will. Martha began to do all sorts of civic projects and became quite accepted. However, it came time to leave Belton.

For some time the group had discussed moving from Belton. It didn't matter that the town found them an asset after so much harassment. They had talked to God, and He would lead them. He led them to Washington, D.C. and a large house that they paid $23,000 for in cash. With its own garden, chicken yard, and orchard, the sisters settled in for the rest of their days. No one cared that the colony was slowly but surely dying out, and no new members were added. They were a group of women who had defied tradition, struck out on their own, and made their way in the world. The sense of self respect these women must have felt was truly magnificent. They had dared to be different and won! If someone else wanted to be sanctified, then let them start their own group.

As for Martha McWhirter, she may have been something of a mystic, but she was also a financial whiz. Figures are vague as to just how much the sisters were worth when they left Belton, but it was probably well over $200,000. Not bad for a lady with visions!

The Circus Queen

It was cotton picking time down in Texas
And the leaves of all the trees a golden brown.
The children and the old folks were happy
For the Mollie Bailey show had come to town.

Author Unknown

H ERE COMES AUNT MOLLIE and her circus! Hurry to the circus lot! They'll be setting up the Big Top soon!" Excitement reached every nook and cranny of those small Texas towns when those magic words were heard. For weeks, the circus was all everyone wanted to talk about. It brought dazzle and glitter to a drab existence. Rare animals from faraway places made young minds yearn to travel to exotic lands, and made their hearts rise in their throats as daring acts were performed by the star acrobats. In a bygone time when entertainment on a wondrous scale was rare indeed, it is no wonder so many kids wanted to run away from home and join the circus. One young lady who did just that ended up making the circus her whole life and brought excitement and glamor to thousands of people who never forgot Mollie Bailey.

Mollie grew up on her father's Alabama plantation with a natural talent for the theatrical and adored the stage during her brief school years. Who knows, Mollie might have gone on to become a great actress, but Mollie fell in love. Her story was like that of a romance novel. Against her father's wishes and without his knowledge, fourteen-year-old Mollie went to see the circus. In the band was a handsome red-headed cornet player, and it was love at first sight. Naturally Mollie's father objected to his beautiful young daughter making such a poor match. So, Mollie ran

**Mollie Bailey
Blum, 1879**

Mollie Bailey, Texas' greatest entertainer, was the only woman to operate a circus.

away from home to marry Gus Bailey. Her father never forgave her, and he never saw his willful daughter again. Even though Mollie returned home several times to make amends, the unrelenting father refused to even see her.

The circus was in Mollie's blood and nothing would stop her from her chosen career. Even the Civil War became a background for this remarkable lady's talents. Gus was the bandmaster for Hood's Texas Brigade, and on the eve of the Second Battle of Manassas he wrote for his comrades "The Old Gray Mare."

Mollie, the consumate actress, fell right in with the role of spy. A little old lady selling cookies behind Federal lines became a young woman dashing on horseback to the Confederate troops with information on the enemy's movements. A dedicated nurse smuggled medicine to her soldiers in gray by hiding it in her elaborate pompadoured hair.

At last the war was over and Gus and Mollie became troopers again. They even did the riverboat circuit. Then the Baileys decided to try a fresh start in Texas with their own circus. They certainly had enough performers, for six of their nine children had survived to have their own part in "A Texas Show for Texas People." In 1879 the Baileys were Texas bound.

Eugene delighted the crowds with his waltzing horses. Allie's acrobatic dogs made the children's faces brighten with laughter. Brad was the exciting and brave highwire man, Minnie sang, and Birda had her "educated" canaries. It was up to Willie to tend to the myriad details of transforming the tent into a magical wonderland. The Baileys staged a good clean family show. No games of chance fleeced the audience, and if one of Mollie's hands ever took a drink or uttered a profane word, he was fired immediately.

Gus's health began to fail and he was unable to keep going on the circuit, but Mollie was a true professional and the circus was her life. There were a lot bigger circuses and perhaps they held more allure, but Mollie Bailey and her thirty-one wagons did more for Texas hometowns than all the large outfits combined.

What a businesswoman she was! Mollie could show modern-day ad men a trick or two when it came to promoting her product. Several days before the circus arrived in town, families would start coming to town to camp out near the circus lot. Then they would watch the lumbering gaily-painted wagons roll in, the strange animals unloaded, and the long-awaited moment when the Big Top went up. Mollie knew how much the preliminaries meant to the small towns to become a part of the show, and it always paid off.

The Civil War was still recent history, and Mollie never forgot her boys in gray. Not only did she fly the American and Lone Star flags, but the Stars and Bars waved over the tent as well. All Confederate veterans were admitted free and recognized for their service to Texas.

When Mollie came to town, this astute woman visited every merchant and bought something. Her purchase might have been something as small as a button or a needle, but "Aunt Mollie" was always there calling each storekeeper by name. The personal touch was her trademark. But Mollie was grateful to her devoted followers in other ways. Often she would donate the proceeds of a certain performance to the church building fund, and scores of small towns in Texas owe their Confederate monument to the generosity of Mollie Bailey.

Another unique touch of this smalltown circus was to purchase its own town lot for its use every year. During the other months Mollie offered the lot to the citizens for their ballgames, barbecues, and community projects. At one time the Bailey Circus owned more than 150 lots. What a great public relations expert this lady was. When the Bailey Circus took to the rails, many little hamlets were left out. It must have broken the hearts of many of Mollie's fans, but she donated her land to the town as a permanent park.

Mollie Bailey was the only woman to ever own and operate a circus, and she did her job very successfully. Yet she never changed her prices in her forty years of touring. Adults got in for thirty-five cents, children twenty-five cents and reserved seats were a dime.

This beautiful woman always kept her love of life and her zest for adventure. In her magnificent clothes and her diamonds, Mollie Bailey found eternal youth. She "believed that laughter and happiness were necessary for the health." What better place for a woman with her outlook than a circus with its thrills and excitement—where everyone is a kid again, no matter what their age. When Mollie died in 1918 at seventy-seven, Texas lost her greatest showman and she has never been replaced.

Only One Life Was Lost

Alfred S. Hayne
Fort Worth, 1890

A S YOU DRIVE THROUGH Fort Worth on busy Interstate 30, give a thought to Alfred S. Hayne, an Englishman by birth who cared more for his fellow man than he did his life. For, underneath this roaring thoroughfare stands an unnoticed marker and monument to a man who sacrificed his life in one momentous act of heroism and courage.

Times were good on the farmlands of Texas in the year 1889, and following a suggestion by General R. A. Cameron, an officer of the Fort Worth and Denver Railway, city promoters developed the idea of an annual exhibition for the display of Texas' bountiful agricultural products. To house a representation of the wealth to be found in North and West Texas, a fabulous exposition building was erected and christened the Spring Palace.

Designed by the Fort Worth firm of Armstrong and Messer, the magnificent wooden structure was 200 feet square and was topped by a massive Moorish dome 110 feet high and 60 feet in diameter. Its roof was covered with cotton. Atop the Spring Palace twelve oriental towers flew flags of the United States and Texas, and each tower was made of different agricultural products of Texas such as grains, cotton, and corn. Grounds were lavishly landscaped in native Texas plants, and even palm trees waved in Fort Worth's breezes.

No expense was spared on the advertising campaign. Special committees traveling in special railroad cars were sent to Washington, D.C., and Mexico City to present invitations to Presidents Harrison and Diaz of the two Republics to attend the Spring Palace's grand opening May 29th, 1889. To set the tone of the elaborate preparations, the invitations were hand painted on silver-washed satin and encased in a casket of highly polished Texas bird's-eye maple.

Before this "unique Karporama" closed on June 20, 1889, the Buffalo Sunday Express stated that, "The Texas Spring Palace will surpass the World's Fair in Paris, France. People who cannot go to Paris this spring might do well to substitute a trip to Fort Worth."

A lot of people did go to Fort Worth in 1889, and when the directors opened the 1890 subscription lists, cities and counties from all over the state were assigned space in the building. Prizes were offered for the most attractive decorations, and one hundred women worked eight to ten hours a day for one hundred days decorating the Spring Palace more beautifully than the year before. Response was so overwhelming, one hundred feet had to be added to the east and west wings.

The second year was very profitable for Fort Worth's new attraction, and the Spring Palace was considered a success from every standpoint. Attendance far exceeded the first year, and plans were underway for each year to be bigger and better than ever. To celebrate the overwhelming victory, the last night was dedicated to a grand fancy dress ball. Special trains were run from surrounding cities and towns, and Dallas alone sent

THE TEXAS SPRING PALACE AT FORT WORTH, TEXAS
OPENS, MAY 29. CLOSES, JUNE 20.
A UNIQUE KARPORAMA–CONSTRUCTED OF AND EXHIBITING THE PRODUCTS OF TEXAS

A horrible holocaust accompanied the closing of Fort Worth's Spring Palace, but only one life was lost in the conflagration. Alfred Hayne died saving others.

more than 1,000 people in their best bib and tucker. May 20, 1890, was to be a memorable evening indeed—but not one of joy and merrymaking.

No sooner had the dance begun when the horror-stricken scream of, "Fire! Fire! Fire!" created pandemonium and terror among the 7,000 guests. In four minutes the building was a mass of flames and in eleven minutes the showplace of Fort Worth was a heap of flaming embers. So rapidly did the blaze spread, firemen did not have time to turn on the fire hydrants.

Miraculously, of the 7,000 lives in danger, 6,999 were spared. Only one life was lost, that of a civil engineer named Alfred Hayne. Hayne was one of the most active and efficient in directing the hurling throngs to one of the sixteen exits. But, his true act of courage was saving the babies of the dancers from the second floor nursery. Hayne gently dropped the infants to the nets waiting below, saving them all.

Fierce flames blocked his escape through the inferno, so the brave engineer was forced to jump. As Haynes hit the ground, both of his ankles were broken. Already badly burned, the unfortunate man was unable to flee the flames raging behind him. A group of gallant men took the fly from a tent that stood in the garden and threw it over the hero, but it was too late. Hayne died of his burns the next day, the only casualty of a night of terror.

No one knows the exact cause of the fire. Frank Leslie's *Illustrated Newspaper* reported, "A boy stepped on a match near the base of a decorated column, and the tiny spark ended in a holocaust." Effort to rebuild the Spring Palace ended in failure because of the economic panic of 1893.

Today hundreds of cars go past this small monument, but none stop to read the story of Al Hayne's sad demise. His brave deed is all but forgotten by a city who owes him so much.

The Seeliger Special

**Emil Seeliger
Lockhart, 1902**

A HOT TEXAS JULY sun was scorching the prairies, and the quiet town of Lockhart was amicably tending to its business. It hadn't been such a very long time ago that gunslingers and outlaws were walking these same streets, but by 1902 life was placid in this small farming community. Suddenly all hell broke loose!

A monster came charging up the streets belching and sputtering, terrorizing the horses and causing sheer havoc! It was the "Seeliger Special"!

The first victim of the Seeliger Special was a delivery wagon loaded with sewing machines. The crazed horses drew the wagon across a pothole and one of the machines flew off and hit a lamppost. Then a fine imported glassed-in carriage with a uniformed driver and a pair of high-stepping horses with red tassels raced out of town at breakneck speed. The kids were absolutely delighted with all the excitement and enchanted with the "Seeliger Special." They couldn't wait for Emil Seeliger to give them a ride in Lockhart's first "hossless wagon."

Seeliger's car was a masterpiece of Rube-Goldberg ingenuity. The ingenious blacksmith had pioneered an automobile the likes of which have never been repeated. This do-it-yourself car may not have been made on the Detroit assembly line, but it certainly made Emil Seeliger famous around Texas.

Try to envision a chassis and body built from an old trap buggy riding on bicycle wheels using single tube casings. The one-cylinder gas engine delivered power to the rear wheels via three bicycle chain drives. Ralph

The "Seeliger Special" rolled the streets of Lockhart terrifying horses and delighting youngsters.

Nader would have had apoplexy if he had seen the gas tank which was also a back rest for the front and only seat. To fill it, Seeliger bought five gallons of gasoline at the drugstore for thirty-five cents a gallon. With a carburetor from an old gasoline-powered boat the two dry cell batteries serving as an ignition system, the "Seeliger Special" sped along at a daring fifteen miles per hour and averaged fourteen miles per gallon. Among this collection of odds and ends on wheels was the steering column—just an old shotgun barrel mounted with bicycle handlebars. To steer, you just pushed the handlebars in the direction you wanted to go.

This innovative German blacksmith spent $125 on his "Special," and his big expense was the $60 for the 4 tubeless tires. Incredibly enough, the Seeliger family ran their "Special" for a number of years, even on the railroad tracks.

The horses may never have accepted "Seeliger's Special," but Lockhart was proud of their hometown inventor. Sadly, however, the "Special" ended up on the junk heap, probably looking right at home there.

Texans like to brag about their "firsts," and Emil Seeliger deserves his plaudits with the first one hundred percent Texas car. There's no doubt about it, Seeliger successfully bridged the gap from blacksmith shop to mechanics shop even before a mechanic's expertise was necessary.

Texas, Our Texas

T exas A&M students thrill to the "Aggie War Hymn," U.T. alumni drawl out "The Eyes of Texas Are Upon You," and everybody knows "The Yellow Rose of Texas" is the most popular girl in the Lone Star State, but few Texans know the melody, much less the lyrics to their state song, "Texas, Our Texas."

**William J. Marsh
Fort Worth, 1924**

Texas, our Texas!
All hail the mighty State!
Texas, our Texas!
So wonderful—so great!
Largest and grandest,
Withstanding every test;
O Empire, wide and glorious,
You stand supremely blest.

The composer of these stirring words, William J. Marsh, was born in Woolton, England, in 1880 of an American mother and British father. Marsh was blessed with a remarkable musical talent and at sixteen replaced his mother as organist for St. Mary's Catholic Church in Woolton.

At twenty-four the young musician was in Fort Worth visiting relatives and was offered a bookkeeping position. Rather than devote his full time to his music, surprisingly Marsh worked for the Neil P. Anderson Company for thirty-five years. But music was Marsh's life, and his every spare minute was spent fulfilling his talent. Not only did Marsh play the organ at Temple Beth-El Synagogue for twenty-three years, for forty-one years he was the organist at his church, St. Patrick's Cathedral. But those were not all of the musician's weekend performances. After playing for ten o'clock mass at St. Patrick's, Marsh dashed frantically to First Presbyterian Church for the eleven o'clock services. This superstar organist also taught at Our Lady of Victory Church and for decades was the music critic for the Fort Worth *Star Telegram*.

You can't help but wonder how Marsh managed to cram so much ability into one lifetime. The teacher, critic, performer, and bookkeeper was yet to do more, much more. He added composing to his list of talents. Marsh wrote and published 125 musical scores. Most were masses and hymns, yet they included the official march for the Texas Centennial Exposition, and Marsh was the first Texan to publish an opera, *The Flower Fair at Peking*.

In 1924 Governor Pat Neff announced a contest to provide Texas with a state song. Neff waxed eloquent in his announcement with references to the "Marseillaise" of France and England's "God Save the King." Neff even quoted an unknown patriot who stated, "Let me write the songs of a people and I care not who makes their laws." As a final inspiration for entries in the contest for a state anthem, the governor offered a prize of $1,000. The $1,000 probably brought in many more entries than the grandiose reference to those "foreign" songs.

Over 400 songs were submitted to the committee, and just before Christmas Neff telephoned Marsh that "Texas, Our Texas" was the state song. Unfortunately, Neff had only a few more days in office, and Governor Miriam Ferguson was not the least interested in her predecessor's cause. "Texas, Our Texas" seemed doomed to be forgotten along with the $1,000 prize money.

About three years later Senator Margie Neal of Carthage, who was a descendant of Francis Scott Key, was appointed to head another committee to select a state song. Another contest was held. Judging took place during the State Fair and for three days the committee listened to over 1,000 paeans to Texas and her glories. Once again "Texas, Our Texas" was the winner.

Finally, on May 23, 1929, Governor Dan Moody signed the bill making it official, and the song was formally presented in a joint session of the legislature on March 1, 1930. The words were sung by soprano Mrs. Pearl Calhoun Davis of Fort Worth. Marsh even received his $1,000, but it had been raised by private subscription, not a grateful legislature.

Naturally there were (and still are) objections that "Texas, Our Texas" isn't "catchy," but John Phillip Sousa declared it was the finest state song he had ever heard. Marsh himself felt, "Such a song is dedicated to the heart and the intelligence, not to the feet." Even though it took five years and three governors, now "Texas, Our Texas" is played at the inauguration of governors, the openings of sessions of the legislature, all official appearances of the governor, and on all occasions when Texas is to be officially recognized as on state holidays and commencement exercises in schools and colleges.

Perhaps "Texas, Our Texas" isn't a melody that keeps going through your head, but all Texans share the sentiments expressed in the chorus:

God bless you, Texas
And keep you brave and strong.
That you may grow in power and worth
Throughout the ages long.

How They Played The Game

For when the One Great Scorer comes
To write against your name,
It matters not if you won or lost,
But how you played the game.

Grantland Rice

THE MASONIC HOME'S MIGHTY Mites played the game like the superstars they were. The year was 1932 and the enveloping gloom of the Great Depression had settled over the country with a vengeance. More than 2,200 banks had failed and there was no money for food and shelter, much less entertainment. Yet, during those dark years a bunch of orphaned boys captured the heart and spirit of thousands of Americans and sparked a ray of hope for better times to come.

The State Championship Class A high school football game was at stake, and the excitement and furor over which team would win was as thrilling as any Cotton Bowl game today. Fort Worth's undefeated Masonic Home's Mighty Mites faced Corsicana's undefeated Tigers. More than 10,000 fans were expected at "one of the greatest battles of the season and every type of play likely to be seen."

Coach "Rusty" Russel of the Mighty Mites wanted to stage the contest at TCU's stadium, but future governor Buford Jester bargained for Corsicana and the Tigers would come to TCU only if they received 75 percent of the gate. To settle the issue, a coin was tossed, and Corsicana won the field. The date was set for December 26. You can just imagine what an anxious Christmas Day it was for the teams, for they well knew this game was the sporting event of the year.

Russel began his fighting team in 1927 with eighty-five boys in four grades as a weak Class B school. Unable to recruit, the only way the

H. N. "Rusty" Russel Fort Worth, 1932

coach could get students was if they were orphaned and placed at Masonic Home. Russel was always out-numbered and out-weighed. His only hope was to out-maneuver and out-fight.

The orphaned boys began to defeat so many Class B schools that their fans demanded their classification be changed. When the undefeated Mighty Mites won the 1931 Class B region by trouncing Clarendon 55-0, it was definitely time for a change.

The Mighty Mites were finally invited into the big Fort Worth District 7A and the boys proved how appropriate their name was by winning over all of their opponents by 224 points to a weak 32.

Next came the Dallas champions, the Woodrow Wilson Wildcats. Their athletic director, P. C. Cobb, was determined to show the Mighty Mites who were the real football heroes. Cobb sent other coaches to scout his opponent, but all was in vain. The Mighty Mites won with an easy 40-7 victory before 10,000 fans in TCU Stadium.

On to the quarter finals! The Mighty Mites rolled over Sherman's Bearcats with a 20-0 win. Then, it was Amarillo and Blair Cherry's Golden Sandstorm. The weather was as ghastly as winter on the high plains can be. Ice, sleet, and freezing temperatures were all against the Fort Worth stars, but teamwork and an intense drive won a hard victory of 7-6.

The only obstacle left in the Mighty Mites' path to the hallowed State Championship was John Pierce's Corsicana Tigers. The Tigers had won 9 and tied 2, with 313 points to 32. One win was a tie won on penetrations as the Tigers had pierced the opponents' twenty-yard line the most times. They were a formidable foe indeed!

The Fort Worth *Star Telegram* printed directions to Corsicana. Highway 34 through Ennis was partially gravel, so the best way was through Dallas and Oak Cliff. KFJZ broadcast the game right after *Lawrence Welk* and before *Amos and Andy.*

What a game! Corsicana had added new grandstands for the game, but so hastily were they built that one grandstand collapsed beneath 2,000 fans. Amazingly, no major injuries were suffered. The *Star Telegram* ran photographs showing play continuing as the crowds pressed forward on the field to the forty-yard line. Neither side could score. It was maddening, not only to the fans, but to the teams. Three times Masonic Home's safety, Bailey Thorpe, fumbled punts, which he had never done before. How could any human being concentrate with 10,000 fans screaming instructions? Here was football at its greatest. When field judge Rosco Minton signalled the end of the game, the Tigers were on the Mighty Mites' one-yard line and the score was 0-0. Sadly, the Mighty Mites still lost. The win was decided by penetrations, and once again Corsicana had triumphed. The long schedule had taken its toll on Russel's team. The coach always played the same eleven boys plus two substitutes, and mighty as they were, even the greatest are human.

The next years were glorious, however, for Russel and his orphans. Out of eleven seasons he won Class A seven times and tied once. Allie White became the only football player ever to make All-State three times. In the very first Cotton Bowl TCU's starting backfield were ex-Mighty Mites Scott McCall, Glenn Roberts, and Harold McClure. Another Mighty Mite that sports fans will recognize was Sweetwater's Slinging Sammy Baugh, probably the greatest college quarterback of the century.

Not all of Russel's boys went on to fame as athletes. Abner McCall became president of Baylor and Jerry Pickett was a district judge. Nor did Rusty spend his entire career at Masonic Home. He moved to Highland Park to coach Doak Walker and Bobby Lane in 1941–1943. Russel came to Highland Park with a reputation as "a young genius whose football teams at the Masonic Home have been a power for years." Last stop in Russel's fantastic career was head coach for SMU.

Rusty Russel died at age 90 in 1983, beloved and worshiped by "his kids." He would have loved his obituary by Dr. Jerry Clem who played with the Mustangs from 1950–1953. "He was one of the first to use things like the spread offense and the shotgun. I thought the world of him." Rusty Russel knew how to play the game.

Supersleuth of Texas History

Louis Wiltz Kemp
Austin, 1932

A STROLL THROUGH THE State Cemetery in Austin is like walking through a *Who's Who in Texas History.* You pass by Elizabeth Ney's magnificent recumbent statue of Albert Sidney Johnston, Coppini's impressive Stephen F. Austin, and many other famous names of those who shaped the destiny of Texas. Every department of the state

The supersleuth of Texas History, Louis Kemp, described himself as merely "an asphalt salesman."

government and every period of Texas history is represented in the cemetery. When General Burleson died in 1851, the state legislature set aside a plot of ground for its honored dead. It was probably inspired by the Congressional cemetery in Washington. There is a special section in this special cemetery with more than 2,000 graves for veterans of the Civil War and their widows.

You may not recognize all of the names on the numerous headstones in this beautiful graveyard, but all have served Texas in their own way. Members and ex-members of the Texas Legislature are allowed burial here as are elected state officials and those appointed by the governor. One exception to this rule was that of the beloved J. Frank Dobie whose interment was by special permission of the governor.

Another exception was Louis Wiltz Kemp. If any Texan deserved honorable burial in the "Arlington of Texas," it is Louis Kemp. "Lou" as he was affectionately called, referred to himself as "a retired asphalt salesman who makes a hobby of Texas history." But, no one was more dedicated to his hobby than Lou Kemp. This supersleuth spent nearly thirty years locating the remains of more than one hundred early-day Texas pioneers and heroes and bringing them to rest in the Texas State Cemetery.

To Lou Kemp, the thought of a Texas patriot lying buried in an unknown or unmarked grave was more than he could bear. Spending his own funds to finance his research and most of his travels, this Sherlock Holmes of Texana made a contribution to Texas history that cannot be measured.

Lou was born in Cameron, Texas, in 1881. In 1908 he went to work for The Texas Company (Texaco) and remained an honored employee until his retirement. Lou traveled extensively throughout the state for Texaco and indulged in his passion for Texas history by searching out neglected and abandoned cemeteries. There he found the names of the great and near-geat in Texas past in their forgotten and sometimes even unmarked graves. It was unforgivable to Lou for a state that owed these men and women so much to have their remains unrecognized. Thus began a statewide hunt on the part of Lou Kemp for the graves of Texas heroes that deserved the honor of being buried in the State Cemetery.

Kemp found the unmarked grave of James W. Henderson in Houston's Glenwood Cemetery who served twenty-one days as Texas' fifth governor. He located Governor Peter Bell in North Carolina; Governor R. H. Runnels, the only man to defeat Houston in a political election; James Pinckney Henderson, Texas' first governor; Jesse Grimes who signed the Declaration of Independence; John A. Greer, Lieutenant Governor in 1845 of Greer County fame; and Robert M. (Three-Legged Willie) Williamson. (Missouri refused to let Moses Austin's remains leave the state.) If the graves were in good condition and not in abandoned cemeteries, Kemp did not move them.

A love of Texas history was not Kemp's only contribution by any means. In 1925 Kemp gained nationwide notice with a one-man crusade against corruption in the state highway commission. Following accusations by him, two commissioners resigned under fire, and a long series of grand jury investigations resulted in a state house-cleaning of highway department procedure and personnel.

Lou was a man who was not satisfied until he had the whole truth. He dug his way into old records and books and diaries until he unearthed numerous unknown facts about Texas. The official state seal had Spanish oak leaves (Heaven forbid!) instead of the originally designed live oak leaves until the master researcher pointed out the error. The seal was immediately changed.

Contrary to popular belief that Crockett died fighting the Mexicans until the bitter end at the Alamo, Kemp proved the Tennessean was actually shot while surrendering to Santa Anna. He located the massacre site and burial place of Fannin's men at Goliad. He was the prime mover in the plan to construct the San Jacinto Monument and Museum and was instrumental in having drives built in the San Jacinto Battleground area so that spots which had been accessible only by foot or on horseback might easily be reached. The names on the great bronze plaque at the monument are the result of Louis Kemp's research, as is his invaluable book *The Heroes of San Jacinto*.

Another of Kemp's proud achievements was that he found the undiscovered important historical data that there were fifty-nine men to sign the Texas Declaration of Independence, not the accepted fifty-eight. His book *The Signers of the Texas Declaration of Independence* is a classic for historians.

Lou was on many of the state's historical committees and was one of the directors of the compilation of the book *Monuments Erected by the State of Texas to Commemorate the Centenary of Texas Independence*. He served long and devotedly to keep the flame of Texas' history burning clearly and honestly. At the time of his death in 1956, Lou had amassed a magnificent collection of Texana, probably one of the best in the entire country.

Kemp had a 1,500-volume library of many books of great rarity and others long out of print. He had amassed biographies on 35,000 Texans and their families from 1821–1845. Lou filled a large vault with irreplaceable periodicals and pamphlets, plus 250 written manuscripts cross-indexed and filed. His research journals of 44 volumes are thorough and accurate. They complement his other work and provide a vivid picture of the life of this truly remarkable Texan. Lou's library and work is priceless because it cannot be recreated. Its authors are gone, as are many of the sources Lou employed.

In March of 1932 in gratitude for Lou Kemp's indefatigable research on its heroes and his service to the state cemetery, the state dedicated the cemetery's paved highway to him. A monument bears a plaque: "The drives of this state cemetery were constructed by the state highway department and dedicated to Louis W. Kemp, whose services made possible the appropriate reburial of many Texas heroes and statesmen or the restoration of their graves. State Board of Control. March, 1932."

Patron Saint of the Soaps

**Albert Lasker
Galveston, 1942**

THE THOUSANDS AND THOUSANDS of fans devoted to television's "soaps" should have as their patron saint Albert Lasker. "The Father of Modern Advertising" created the first soap opera on the airwaves way back in the twenties with *The Story of Mary Marlin.* Mary Marlin's trials and tribulations probably seem insignificant compared to those shown on television today, but Mary was a smashing success.

The first soap opera was not Lasker's only claim to fame by any means. When this young Galvestonian came to Lord & Thomas Advertising Agency in Chicago at the turn of the century, The Borden Company's advertising budget was $513.75 and Wrigley's was $32 annually. For that, Borden and Wrigley got ads in a few newspapers. Lasker would end up owning Lord & Thomas and retire forty-four years later with the agency worth $45 million by his ideas alone.

Born in Galveston in 1880, Lasker began his promotional career at the age of twelve with his own newspaper, a four-page weekly called the *Galveston Free Press.* At sixteen the young genius was writing Congressman R. B. Hawley's speechs and acting as his campaign manager. The next year Lasker launched Jack Johnson, the first black heavyweight champion, on his rise to fame. Obviously Galveston was too small for this brilliant young entrepreneur.

At Lord & Thomas Lasker found his true calling—advertising. In 1911 he made Palmolive the best selling soap in America by telling women the green soap with the green and black label would "keep that schoolgirl complexion." Next, Lasker took Quaker Oats' Wheat Berries and Puffed Berries cereals and had them "shot from guns" into Puffed Rice and Puffed Wheat.

Back when smoking was in vogue, Lasker told America "to reach for a Lucky instead of a sweet." When this brought down the wrath of American candy manufacturers, the slogan was changed to "Reach for a Lucky instead."

Lasker's success with Kleenex, Frigidaire, and Studebaker was also phenomenal. Not only did this great ad man put "Irium" into Pepsodent, Lasker put Bob Hope on its radio show and sales soared.

Millions of Americans were dedicated listeners of other Lasker programs such as *Your Hit Parade, Information, Please,* and *Mr. District Attorney.* On a summer evening you could stroll around the block and never miss a word of the most popular show on the air, *Amos and Andy.*

Tense and dynamic, Lasker even left his hospital bed for a meeting, so one story goes. After the meeting he closed with, "Gentlemen, I have done all I can for you. Now I must return to Johns Hopkins and continue my nervous breakdown." The world's greatest salesman once called his staff in for a short speech and ended it three days later. It should come as no surprise that when Lasker retired he was a multimillionaire.

Albert Lasker and his wife, Mary, rendered their country a great service during World War II. In 1942 Mary became fascinated with a book *Victory Through Air Power* by Major de Seversky. At this time Roosevelt was dominated by his admirals who scoffed at air power, and the United States was not taking a realistic view of the might of the airplane. Mary bought 200 copies of the book and pressured her husband and friends into reading Seversky's views.

Many people thought Seversky was a crank, but Lasker saw him as a genius. This Russian Bolshevik was a pioneer in aircraft and advocated long range bombers as more effective than a battleship. Lasker, who knew everybody, arranged for Seversky to meet Frank Knox, Secretary of the Navy and Donald Nelson of the War Production Boards. It was Albert Lasker that gave Seversky backing, confidence, and hope. He coined the phrase, "The longer the range, the shorter the war."

Walt Disney made *Victory Through Air Power* into a film with Seversky writing the script, but Roosevelt refused to watch it. Then at the Quebec meeting in 1943 Churchill asked Roosevelt if he had seen the movie. A print was immediately flown in, and the two great leaders watched it together. FDR had the Joint Chiefs take a look at the film, and it played an important role in getting D-Day sufficient air power. Because of Seversky, the B-29 was born.

Years later Lasker heard the details and was very pleased. It moved him profoundly that Mary had pressured his interest in Seversky and he had played an indirect role in saving many American lives.

The last ten years of Lasker's life were spent amassing a magnificent private art collection and on his and Mary's favorite charity, the American Cancer Society. This was long before research proved smoking was directly linked to cancer; in fact, it was lack of research that prompted this generous couple to dedicate their energy to the American Cancer Society. Albert's mother had died of cancer, and her son found out that not only was very little known about the disease but that very little research had been done. With his incredible energy, Lasker decided to change all that.

When Albert and Mary became involved with the American Cancer Society in 1943, the organization had never raised more than $350,000 a year. Albert took over the fund drive with the stipulation that at least one-fourth of the money raised be used for research. Before, the American Cancer Society had only spent money on pamphlets informing the public of their project and the symptoms of the disease. To even use the word "cancer" on the radio was taboo, and Albert Lasker set out to change such medieval concepts.

With the help of such stars as Bob Hope and Fibber McGee and Molly more than $4 million was raised. Because of his super salesmanship Lasker took the wraps off of cancer and made it less mysterious and terrifying. For his work with the American Cancer Society alone, Albert Lasker would qualify as a great unsung hero, but his life was too full to be satisfied with only one project.

Lasker loved to scout out and discover new enterprises and give money unasked. He was tremendously interested in anybody with talent. This man who was fond of people filled his world with a variety of men and women. Albert Lasker was truly the "greatest salesman in the world." At his death, by cancer, Mary had 250 cherry trees, and 50,000 daffodils planted in his memory at the United Nations building in New York.

Mr. Wildflowers

**Carroll Abbott
Kerrville, 1984**

WHEN YOU MEET SOME people, you know immediately they are special. Such was the case when my friend Kathryn Walker introduced me to Carroll Abbott. I knew I had met a very special person indeed.

It was a frantic May 31, 1983. I had opened my country inn and restaurant for the very first time for Kathryn's wildflower tour. Needless to say, I was in a state of panic, having never owned or operated a restaurant before, but I had to make time to talk to Mr. Wildflowers himself, Carroll Abbott.

We stood on the back deck of my 1891 Badu House and talked about the yard. Carroll had marvelous ideas of how it should be landscaped using native plants, and I was bemoaning the fact that the restoration costs had been so high, there was nothing left over for doing the grounds. Then I found myself talking about my fears of failure in this unknown venture, my hopes and dreams for The Badu House and I virtually bared my soul to a man I had only just met. But Carroll was the kind of person that you trusted immediately. I've never forgotten his advice, "Sure, Ann, it's going to be rough, and you'll make a lot of mistakes, but never give up. No matter what, just never give up, and you'll be a success." Before he left, Carroll gave me a copy of his *How to Know and Grow Texas Wildflowers*. It was the first thing stolen from The Badu House.

I didn't see Carroll for a long time. We called and wrote occasionally but could never get together. I still treasure the note he sent me in January of 1984: "Good Person, I wish you well in 1984 and I want you to grab hold of something—anything!—and hang in there. Success takes time. Grow good! Carroll"

Finally, one beautiful spring day of that year, Carroll came driving up to have lunch at my restaurant. It was so wonderful to see him again. He was on his way to Dallas, for the success he had been striving for was on the horizon. He had been called in as a consultant for both Trammel Crow and Ross Perot. They had some mammoth projects going and needed Carroll's expertise on landscaping.

But, Carroll did not look well. His features were bloated, and he moved so slowly. He had had a reoccurrence, which in the jargon of cancer patients, meant he had cancer again. He talked about the new treatment and his hopes for the experimental drugs they were trying. This was the first time he had been out or felt like driving in weeks. He was driving up the backroads to Dallas because he wanted to check the roads where some special flowers grew.

Just as big things were finally breaking for him, cancer had struck again, for the third time. I offered the usual platitudes about how I was sure his treatment would work, but we both knew his odds of winning this round were not good. Yet, Carroll had such a peaceful resigned air about him, as if to say, "Yes, I've been dealt some really bad luck, but I'll handle it." I truly marveled at his lack of bitterness.

Carroll Abbott's zest for life and love of nature made him truly Texas' "Mr. Wildflowers."

I saw Mr. Wildflowers one more time before he died. It was at the autograph party for the Highway Department's book *Texas in Bloom*. The two people who love Texas wildflowers more than anyone else were honored guests, Lady Bird Johnson and Carroll Abbott. I didn't have to ask Carroll how he felt. It showed. He was having difficulty walking and standing, and he was very tired and in pain, but he certainly wasn't complaining. We talked instead about his successful meeting with the two business magnates in Dallas.

Carroll wasn't always an authority on wildflowers. He had always loved them, but he had been a newspaper man in his younger days, and a very good one. Then, when he helped out a friend who was running for office, Carroll switched to the more glamorous field of politics. He even ran for office himself, but he was soundly defeated. He wrote a book about his experiences: *The Care and Feeding of Political Volunteers* is a classic. His list of political clients was very impressive, however: John Connally, Ray Roberts, and Ben Barnes.

Just as Carroll reached the top of the ladder and was earning more than $80,000 a year, he gave up the world of politics to grow wildflowers and promote the use of native plants in landscaping. Pat, his wife, was in shock, but if that was what Carroll wanted, she would help him. Those years were really rough, but the Abbotts survived.

In order to make money while advocating the preservation and cultivation of his beloved wildflowers, Carroll tried publishing a wildflower calendar. It took two years and lots of hours by the side of the road to sell those 10,000 calendars. He told the story of how he was sitting by the highway with his calendars, and a man drove by, stopped, got out, and gave him $1,000 with the remark, "I like what you're doing."

In 1978 Carroll decided to write a bestseller, *How to Know and Grow Texas Wildflowers*. After he ran an ad, the orders poured in. So then he wrote it. He lost his manuscript in a flood, and then the bookstores refused to buy his work. Finally, with mail orders, Carroll paid his printing bill for 5,000 copies in 1981.

It was also in the spring of 1981 that Carroll's landscaping company, Green Horizons, began to move to the black side of the ledger. Also, after a lot of politicking and hard work, Carroll managed to get the state to proclaim a Texas Wildflower Day to be celebrated on the weekend before San Jacinto Day. This dedicated man was honored in a joint session of the Texas Legislature for his beautification work and help with the state's wildflower program.

Just when life was becoming as beautiful as the wildflowers he loved, Carroll's luck ran out again. His first bout with lung cancer proved successful, but only temporarily. Carroll Abbott died in 1984 when the wildflowers were in bloom. Yet, he left behind more beauty for his beloved Texas than all the statues, poetry, or music ever written about the Lone Star State. As you drive the Texas highways and backroads and delight in the gorgeous fields with their vibrant colors, think of Carroll Abbott for helping to keep them there. For all Carroll really wanted out of life was for everyone to love the natural beauty of Texas as devotedly as he did.

Index